Textile Finishing
Basic Concepts and Application

The Authors

P. Vinayagamurthi is the Head of Department of Costume Design and Fashion at Sri Jayendra Saraswathy Maha Vidhyalaya College of Arts and Science, Coimbatore. He has spent over 24 years in the industry and his experience includes garment pattern development and industrial engineering. He also has 12 years of experience in Academic. He currently pursues his PhD in Textile Technology at Bharathiar University, Coimbatore. He has a keen interest in developing industrially relevant applications for pattern development. He has published 5 articles in National and 2 in International Journals to his credit and has presented 5 papers in National and 2 in International Conferences. He has delivered special lectures and attended Faculty development programmes conducted by other colleges/universities. He has organized and conducted international conference and many workshops.

Dr. S. Kavitha, Associate Professor & Head, Department of Home Science, Mother Teresa Women's University. She has a doctorate in Textiles and Clothing and her work is on Textile finishing and Medical Textiles. She has 15 years of teaching and two years of industrial experience. Her areas of special interest are Specialty textiles, apparel designing, surface ornamentation and apparel manufacturing. She has organized and conducted workshops, training programs, short term courses and intercollegiate fest. She participated and presented papers in National and International conferences / seminars and published research papers in reputed journals. She has also under taken funded project and has organized training programs funded by Govt. of Tamilnadu. She held additional positions as Member in Board of Studies for various autonomous colleges and universities.

D. Gopalakrishnan is an M.Tech (Textile Chemistry), M.Sc. (Costume Design & Fashion) and MBA (Technology Management) qualified Textile Technologist. Currently working as Project staff at Department of Fashion Technology, PSG College of Technology, Coimbatore. He has 7 years of consolidated teaching experience in various levels of educational institutions and 5 years of industrial experience. He has presented several papers & posters in various National & International conferences in all over India and also has several technical articles published in national, international journals & Textile magazines to his credit. He has also published five books.

Textile Finishing
Basic Concepts and Application

P. Vinayagamurthi

S. Kavitha

D. Gopalakrishnan

2018

Daya Publishing House®

A Division of

Astral International Pvt. Ltd.
New Delhi – 110 002

Published by   : **Daya Publishing House®**
A Division of
Astral International Pvt. Ltd.
– ISO 9001:2015 Certified Company –
4736/23, Ansari Road, Darya Ganj
New Delhi-110 002
Ph. 011-43549197, 23278134
E-mail: info@astralint.com
Website: www.astralint.com

Foreword

This book is an enthusiastic celebration of textile finishing, especially those which are of basic concepts and application relevance. It is also a unique tribute to the students and academicians who were involved in their study. Still another element is provided by many interesting machinery details and an abundance of meaningful illustrations. On top of that, there are innumerable that interweave basics and applications in a very appealing way. Although the emphasis of this work is on textile finishing, it contains much that will be of interest to those outside this field and students of textiles indeed to anyone with a fascination with the world of textile processing.

The authors have selected well five prominent units wise as the key subjects of their essays and contents. Although these represent only a small sample of the world of textile processing, they amply illustrate the importance of this field of textile finishing and the way in which the field has evolved. I think that the authors can be confident that there will be many grateful readers who will have gained a perspective of the disciplines of textile chemical processing and this book as a result of their efforts.

The authors demonstrate clearly the impact we can have on our own destiny through this work. Their book destined to play a major role in exciting, motivating and educating the generation of textile technologist and researchers from all over the textile sector who are bound to make this dream a reality. I strongly recommend this book to the textile students and the faculty who mentor them.

Mrs. C. Premalatha
Professor and Head
Department of Textile Chemistry and Technology
SSM College of Engineering
Komarapalayam, Namakkal – 638 183, Tamilnadu, INDIA

Preface

The units of our *Textile Finishing: Basic Concepts and Application* textbook adhere to the scope and sequence followed by most two-semester in textile science courses nationwide. The development choices for this textbook were made with the guidance of faculty who are deeply involved in teaching this course. These choices led to innovations in finishing, terminology, career applications, practical orientation and modern source of learning, all with a goal of increasing relevance to students.

The unit one provides students with a basic understanding of basic finishing and some of the important finishes applied to textile fabric. These chapters provide a foundation for the further study of the book. They also focus particularly on how the finishing on, important chemicals, and maintain conditions.

In the second unit, students explore the Finishing processes include preparatory treatments used before additional treatment following a traditional sequence of topics. This unit is the first to walk students through specific finishes, and as it does so, it maintains a focus on mechanical finishes as well as heat setting and other treatments.

The Unit three helps the students integrated into deep on the functional finishes and also offers students a unique approach to understanding finishes.

In unit four, examine the principle means of special purpose finishes and also highlights on silicones for multifunctional finishing, micro/ macro/ nano finishing and water repellent finishing.

The closing unit examines the modern finishing technology and systems, describe the process of material development and the different stages of application, and end with a review of the mechanisms.

We strove to make the textile discipline meaningful and memorable to students, so that they can draw from it a knowledge that will enrich their studies.

Mr. P. Vinayagamurthi
Dr. S. Kavitha
Mr. D. Gopalakrishnan

Contents

Classification of Finishes

1.1. Introduction

Textile Finishing is a process used in manufacturing of fiber, fabric, or clothing. In order to impart the required functional properties to the fiber or fabric, it is customary to subject the material to different type of physical and chemical treatments. For example wash and wear finish for a cotton fabric is necessary to make it crease free or wrinkle free. In a similar way, mercerizing, singeing, flame retardant, water repellent, water proof, antistatic finish, peach finish etc are some of the important finishes applied to textile fabric.

1.2. Production sequence and flow chart of wet processing

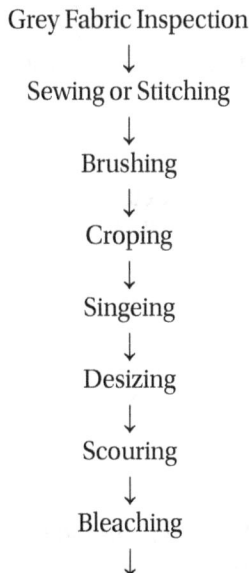

Grey Fabric Inspection
↓
Sewing or Stitching
↓
Brushing
↓
Croping
↓
Singeing
↓
Desizing
↓
Scouring
↓
Bleaching
↓

Mercerizing

↓

Dyeing

↓

Printing

↓

Finishing

↓

Final Inspection

↓

Delivery

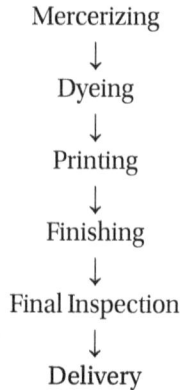

In which way grey fabric is dyed is called wet process technology. Normally wet processing depends on buyer's demand. Suppose buyer wants the more precised dyed fabric. The fabric should mercerise during the dyeing pre-treatment process. Basically the buyer don't want that mercerised fabric there is no need to mercerize your fabric.

Grey fabric inspection

After manufacturing fabric it is inspected in an inspection Table. It is the process to remove neps, warp end breakage, weft end breakage, hole spot.

Stitching

To increase the length of the fabric for making suitable for processing is called stitching. It is done by plain sewing m/c.

Brushing

To remove the dirt, dust, loose fibre & loose ends of the warp & weft threads is known as brushing.

Shearing / Cropping

The process by which the attached ends of the warp & weft thread is removed by cutting by the knives or blades is called shearing. Shearing is done for cotton & cropping for jute. After Shearing or cropping fabrics goes under singeing process.

Singeing

The process by which the protruding / projecting fibres are removed from the fabrics by burning / heat to increase the smoothness of the fabric is called singeing. If required both sides of fabric are singed.

Desizing

The process by which the sizing mtls (starch) are removed from the fabric is known as desizing. This must be done before printing.

Scouring

The process by which the natural impurities (oil, wax, fat etc) & added/external/adventitious impurities (dirt, dust etc) are removed from the fabric is called scouring. It is done by strong NaOH.

Souring

The process by which the alkali are removed from the scoured fabric with dilute acid solution is known as souring.

Bleaching

The process by which the natural colours (nitrogenous substance) are removed from the fabric to make the fabric pure & permanent white is known as bleaching. It is done by bleaching agent.

Mercerizing

The process by which the cellulosic mtls/substance are treated with highly conc.NaOH to impart some properties such as strength, absorbency capacity, lusture is known as mercerizing. It is optional. If the fabrics are 100% export oriented then it is done by highly conc. NaOH (48-52° Tw). Mercerization is one of the most important of all cotton finishes. This finish imparts luster to the cotton, increases its strength by nearly 25% and improves dye affinity, producing brighter shades than unmercerized cotton. It also enhances the hand as well as uses less dye to achieve the same depth of shade. The finish consists of treating the material while under tension with cold, concentrated sodium hydroxide solution. Both fabrics and yarns can be mercerized, but fibres cannot. Mercerization is a permanent finish.

Dyeing

A process of coloring fibers, yarns, or fabrics with either natural or synthetic dyes.

Printing

A process for producing a pattern on yarns, warp, fabric, or carpet by any of a large number of printing methods. The color or other treating material, usually in the form of a paste, is deposited onto the fabric which is then usually treated with steam, heat, or chemicals for fixation.Then finishing treatment are done according to buyer requirements and then folding, packaging, and at last delivery.

1.2.1. Pre-treatment processes

Pre-treatment processes consist of cleaning operations to rid the fabric of all soil and additives used during the weaving or knitting process. These processes are usually the first treatments a fabric undergoes after leaving the loom or knitting machine and are required before any dyeing, printing or finishing can be accomplished. The processes consist of various types of cleaning actions, depending upon the fibre, the impurities present and the fabric construction. In cottons, cotton blend, silk and man-made fibres, the processes are, known generally as the boil-off. In woolens and worsteds, it is called a scour or scouring.

1.3.   Textile Finishing

Finishing is the general term for a multitude of processes and treatments which a fabric may undergo after it has been made (woven or knitted) and coloured (dyed or printed). Textile finishing is a term commonly applied to different process that the textile material under go after pretreatment, dyeing or printing for final embellishment to enhance their attractiveness and sale appeal as well as for comfort and usefulness. It is the final processing of the cloth and its purpose is to make the fabric suitable for its intended end use. That may mean. for example, making the fabric shrinkproof, softer, stiffer, water repellent, crease resistant or a combination of these properties.

1.3.1.   Objects of Finishing:

The aim of finishing is to render textile goods fit for their purpose or end use. Besides that, finishing can be done for achieving the following purposes-

a) To improve fabric attractiveness

- ❖ By modification of fabric appearance (Calendaring, Optical brightening)
- ❖ By altering fabric handle (Softening, Stiffening)
- ❖ Control of fabric dimension (Sanforizing, Compacting)

b) To improve service ability

- ❖ Protection of fabric (Flame proofing, Water proofing)
- ❖ Improved performance (Water repellency, Raising)
- ❖ Easy care properties (Resin finish, Crease recovery)

1.4.   Classification of Finishing

Textile finishes and finishing are classified in several ways. Persons concerned with end products (designers, merchandisers and sales personnel) usually categorize finishes as aesthetic finishes and functional finishes. The former modify the appearance and/or hand (feel) of fabrics, while the latter improve the performance of a fabric under specific end use conditions. Persons concerned with textile processing (chemists and finishers) categorize finishes into chemical finishes and mechanical finishes. These are also called wet finishing and dry finishing, respectively. Finishes are also categorized by their degree of permanence. These finishes are called permanent, durable, semi-durable and temporary.

Permanent finishes usually involve a chemical change in fibre structure and will not change or alter throughout the life of a fabric.

Durable finishes usually last throughout the life of the article, but effectiveness becomes diminished after each cleaning, and near the end of the normal use life of the article, the finish is nearly removed.

Semi-durable finishes last through several launderings or dry cleanings and many are renewable in home laundering or dry cleaning.

Temporary finishes are removed or substantially diminished the first time an article is laundered or dry cleaned. Generally there are two types of finishing. Those are

1. Physical/Mechanical.
2. Chemical.

Physical / Mechanical Finishing

Mechanical Finishes usually involved specific physical treatment to a fabric surface to cause a change in fabric appearance. This is also known as dry finish. It's two types

1. Temporary

A finish which is not stable and goes off after the first wash is known as temporary finish and these finishes disappears during subsequent washing and usage.(Calendaring, embossing, Starching, Softening *etc.*)

Physical or mechanical finishes

These types of finishing treatments include

- ❖ Calendering
- ❖ Sanforising
- ❖ Raising
- ❖ Compating
- ❖ Napping
- ❖ Shearing
- ❖ Sueding
- ❖ Setting and heat-setting

2. Permanent/Durable

If the finishing effect in the fabric does not disappear and remains unaffected through all the conditions of wear and washing treatments, then the finish is said to be permanent finish. (Raising, Sanforizing, *etc.*)

1.4.1. Mechanical Finishing

Involving the application of physical principles such as friction, temperature, pressure, tension and many others.

Calendering

Calendering is not a single type of finish. There are various types of calender machinery, each producing different types of finished fabrics. Fundamentally, a calendar is a mechanical device consisting of two or more large rotating cylindrical rollers stacked on top of each other and usually heated. The cylindrical rollers are in contact with each other under pressure. Fabric being calendared passes around and between these cylinders. The specific type of calendared finished fabric varies with the nature of the cylinder surface, the speed of the cylinders and the nature of the fabric being finished. The various types of calendaring finishes include the following:

a) **Simple calendaring**
b) **Glazing calendaring**
c) **Embossed calendaring**
d) **Moire calendaring**
e) **Schreiner calendaring**

A process of passing cloth between calendar rollers, usually under carefully controlled heat and pressure, to produce a variety of surface textures or effects in fabric such as compact, smooth, supple, flat and glazed. The process involves passing fabric through a calendar in which a highly polished, usually heated, steel bowl rotates at a higher surface speed than the softer (e.g. cotton or paper packed) bowl against which it works, thus producing a glaze on the face of the fabric that is in contact with the steel bowl. The friction ratio is the ratio of the peripheral speed of the faster steel bowl to that of the slower bowl and is normally in the range 1.5 to 3.0. The normal woven fabric surface is not flat, particularly in ordinary quality plain weave fabrics, because of the round shape of the yarns, and interlacings of warp and weft at right angles to each other. In such fabrics it is more often seen that even when the fabric is quite regular, it is not flat. During calendering, the yarns in the fabric are squashed into a flattened elliptical shape; the intersections are made to close-up between the yarns. This causes the fabric surface to become flat and compact. The improved planeness of surface in turn improves the glaze of the fabric. The calender machines may have several rollers, some of which can be heated and varied in speed, so that in addition to pressure a polishing action can be exerted to increase lustre.

Compacting

Durable finish imparted on man-made fibres and knitted fabrics by employing heat and pressure to shrink them to produce a crepy and bulky texture.

Embossing

This particular type of calendering process allows engraving a simple pattern on the fabric.To produce a pattern in relief by passing fabric through a calendar in which a heated metal bowl engraved with the pattern works against a relatively soft bowl, built up of compressed paper or cotton on a metal centre.

Sueding

This process is carried out by means of a roller coated with abrasive material. The fabric has a much softer hand and an improved insulating effect thanks to the fibre end pulled out of the fabric surface.

Raising or Napping

Napping is a mechanical finish in which woven or knitted fabrics are passed against rotating, bristled wire-covered brushes. This action results in fibres actually being raised from the fabric. The overall effect is a fabric with raised fibre surface. The raising of the fibre on the face of the goods by means of teasels or rollers covered with card clothing (steel wires) that are about one inch in height. Action by either method raises the protruding fibres and causes the finished fabric to provide greater warmth to the wearer, makes the cloth more compact, causes the fabric to become softer in hand or smoother in feel; increase durability and covers the minute areas between the interlacings of the warp and the filling. Napped fabrics include blankets, flannel, unfinished worsted, and several types of coatings and some dress goods. Other names for napping are Gigging, Genapping, Teaseled, Raised. Napped fabrics have a softer hand and provide better insulation than the same materials unnapped because they can entrap more air; hence, their wide use in blankets, sleepwear and winter clothing. However, the insulating value of cotton and rayon napped fabrics is not long lasting. The low resilience of these fibres causes premature flattening of the fibre nap. The nap can partially be restored by frequent brushing.

Wool Glazing

This is done on a special machine, which is used to perform functional finishing on wool fabrics after raising.

Shearing

Shearing is an important preparatory stage in the processing of cotton cloth. The objective of Shearing is to remove fibres and loose threads from the surface of the fabric, thus improving surface finish. Shearing is a process used to cut off surface fibres on fabrics. It makes uniform the surface of napped fabrics. Most cut pile fabrics are also sheared to provide uniform pile height.

Stabilization

A term usually referring to fabrics in which the dimensions have been set by a suitable preshrinking operation

Decating

A finishing process applied to fabrics to set the material, enhance lustre and improve the hand. Fabric wound onto a perforated roller is immersed in hot water or has steam blown through it.

Steaming and Heat setting

It is done by using high temperatures to stabilize fabrics containing polyester, nylon, or triacetate but not effective on cotton or rayon.it may be performed in fabric form or garment form it may cause shade variation from side-to-side if done prior to dyeing; may change the shade if done after dyeing

Sanforizing or Pre Shrinking

Sanforizing is a process whereby the fabric is run through a sanforizer; a machine that has drums filled with hot steam. This process is done to control the shrinkage of the fabric.The fabric is given an optimum dimensional stability by applying mechanic forces and water vapour.

Fulling

The structure, bulk and shrinkage of wool are modified by applying heat combined with friction and compression. Fulling is a permanent finish used on wool fabrics; it is also known as milling or felting. The process is a carefully controlled scouring or laundering process to induce felting shrinkage in wool fabrics. The resultant fulled fabric is smoother, more compact and has yarns more tightly embedded than an unfulled fabric. Woolens are frequently heavily fulled.

Plisse

Plisse is the name of a finish as well as the name of a fabric treated with this finish. It is a permanent finish, produced on cotton by the action of sodium hydroxide; but unlike mercerizing, no tension is used. The sodium hydroxide is printed on the fabric in the form of a paste.The fabric shrinks only where the sodium hydroxide is applied, producing a puckered effect.

1.4.2. Chemical Finishing

The finishes applied by means of chemicals of different origins, a fabric can receive properties otherwise impossible to obtain with mechanical means. Finishes obtained by deposition of chemicals such as starch china clay, oil, fats and waxes, synthetic resins, rubber latex, cellulose acetate, cellulose ethers, optical bleaching agents and so on. Finishes obtained by chemical reactions with fibre. These includes-

- ❖ Parchmentising
- ❖ Anti-soil
- ❖ Wrinkle free
- ❖ Anti-crease
- ❖ Wash & wear
- ❖ Durable press
- ❖ Flame retardant
- ❖ Fluorochemical
- ❖ Deodorant & Antimicrobial

❖ Ultraviolet Protection

❖ Enzymes washing

Softening

Softening is carried out when the softness characteristics of a certain fabric must be improved, always carefully considering the composition and properties of the substrate.

Elastomeric Finishes

Elastomeric finishes are also referred to as stretch or elastic finishes and are particularly important for knitwear. These finishes are currently achieved only with silicone-based products. The main effect is durable elasticity, because not only must extensibility be enhanced, but recovery from deformation is of crucial importance. After all stresses and disturbing forces have been released, the fabric should return to its original shape.

Crease Resistant or Crease Proofing

Crease Resistant Finishes are applied to cellulose fibres (cotton, linen and rayon) that wrinkle easily. Permanent Press fabrics have crease resistant finishes that resist wrinkling and also help to maintain creases and pleats throughout wearing and cleaning. Crease resistant finishes are popularly known as CRF finishes. They are used on cotton, rayon and linen because these three fibres wrinkle easily. CKF finishes are resin finishes; the fabric is saturated with resin and then the resin is cured at temperatures of about 360°F. The fabric becomes stiffer, less absorbent and more resistant to wrinkling. Resin treatments also results in tensile strength loss and reduction of abrasion resistance in cellulosic fibres. Most CRF finishes are durable.

Soil Release Finishes

These finishes attract water to the surface of fibres during cleaning and help remove soil. Soil release finishes in fabrics permit relatively easy removal of soils (especially oily soils) with ordinary home laundering. There are several types of soil release finishes. All of them accomplish the end result of making the fibre more absorbent (hydrophilic), thus permitting better "wettability" for improved soil removal. Most soil release finishes are applied at the same time that the resins are applied to textiles. Most are durable through 40 to 50 launderings and are routinely applied to fabrics for work clothes and table cloths. They are also often applied to fabrics for slacks and skirts. Several other benefits arise from the use of soil release finishes in durable press fabrics because of their increased absorbency. These include: improved antistatic properties, improved fabric drapability and somewhat greater comfort in hot weather.

Flame Retardant Treatment

Are applied to combustible fabrics used in children's sleepwear, carpets and curtains and prevent highly flammable textiles from bursting into flame. There are two systems to make fabrics flame resistant. The first is to use selective fibres which have characteristic flame resistant properties. The second is by the use of flame resistant finishes. All of the many types of flame retardant finishes now available suffer from at least one of the following shortcomings : (a) they cause stiffening and loss of fabric drapability; (b) they result in significant strength loss in fabric; (c) they are easily removed in laundering (nondurable); and (d) they become ineffective when laundered in household bleach, with soaps or with water softeners.

Peach finish

Subjecting the fabric (either cotton or its synthetic blends) to emery wheels, makes the surface velvet like. This is a special finish mostly used in garments.

Anti Pilling

Pilling is a phenomenon exhibited by fabrics formed from spun yarns (yarns made from staple fibres). Pills are masses of tangled fibres that appear on fabric surfaces during wear or laundering. Fabrics with pills have an unsightly appearance and an unpleasant handle. Loose fibres are pulled from yarns and are formed into spherical balls by the frictional forces of abrasion. These balls of tangled fibres are held to the fabric surface by longer fibres called anchor fibres. Anti pilling finish reduces the forming of pills on fabrics and knitted products made from yarns with a synthetic-fibre content, which are inclined to pilling by their considerable strength, flexibility and resistance to impact. Anti pilling finish is based on the use of chemical treatments which aim to suppress the ability of fibres to slacken and also to reduce the mechanical resistance of synthetic fibre.

Non Slip Finish

A finish applied to a yarn to make it resistant to slipping and sliding when in contact with another yarn.The main effect of non-slip finishes is to increase the adhesion between fibres and yarns regardless of fabric construction, the generic term for these finishes would be fibre and yarn bonding finishes. Other terms that can be used include anti-slip, non-shift and slip-proofing finishes.

Stain and Soil Resistant Finishes

Prevent soil and stains from being attracted to fabrics. Such finishes may be resistant to oil-boure or water-bourne soil and stains or both. Stain and soil resistant finishes can be applied to fabrics used in clothing and furniture. Scotchgard is a stain and soil resistant finish commonly applied to carpet and furniture.

Oil and Water Proofing

Waterproof Finishes -Allows no water to penetrate, but tend to be uncomfortable because they trap moisture next to the body. Recently, fabrics have been developed that are waterproof, yet are also breathable

Water-Repellent Finishes

Water-repellent finishes resist wetting. If the fabric becomes very wet, water will eventually pass through. Applied to fabrics found in raincoats, all-weather coats, hats, capes, umbrellas and shower curtains.

Absorbent Finishes

Increase fibres' moisture holding power. Such finishes have been applied to towels, cloth diapers, underwear, sports shirts and other items where moisture absorption is important.

Anti Static Finish

Reduce static electricity which may accumulate on fibres. The most common type of anti-static finishes are fabric softeners.

Anti Mildew

In certain ambient (humidity and heat) conditions, cellulose can be permanently damaged. This damage can be due to depolymerisation of the cellulose or to the fact that certain microoganisms (mildews) feed off it. The situation is worsened, during long storage periods, by the presence of starch finishing agents. This damage can be prevented by the use of antiseptics, bacteria controlling products containing quaternary ammonium salts, and phenol derivatives. Dyestuffs containing heavy metals can also act as antiseptics. Permanent modification of the fibre (cyanoethylation) is another possibility.

Mothproofing Finishes

Protect protein-containing fibres, such as wool, from being attacked by moths, carpet beetles and other insects.

Antibacterial Finish

The inherent properties of textile fibres provide room for the growth of micro-organisms. The structure and chemical process may induce the growth, but it is the humid and warm environment that aggravates the problem further. Antimicrobial finish is applied to textile materials with a view to protect the wearer and textile substrate itself. Antimicrobial finish provides the various benefits of controlling the infestation by microbes, protect textiles from staining, discoloration, and quality deterioration and prevents the odor formation. Anti-microbial agents can be applied to the textile substrates by exhaust, pad-dry-cure, coating, spray and foam techniques. The application of the finish is now extended to textiles used for outdoor, healthcare sector, sports and leisure. UV Protection Fabric treated with UV absorbers ensures that the clothes deflect the harmful ultraviolet rays of the sun, reducing a person's UVR exposure and protecting the skin from potential damage. The extent of skin protection required by different types of human skin depends on UV radiation intensity and distribution with reference to geographical location, time of day, and season. This protection is expressed as SPF (Sun Protection Factor), higher the SPF value better is the protection against UV radiation.

Colorfastness Improving Finish

Colour fastness is the resistance of a material to change in any of its colour characteristics, to the transfer of its colourants to adjacent materials or both. Fading means that the colour changes and lightens. Bleeding is the transfer of colour to a secondary, accompanying fibre material. This is often expressed as soiling or staining meaning that the accompanying material gets soiled or stained.The physical and chemical principles involved in the performance of the fastnessnimproving finishes concern either the interaction with the dyestuff or with the fibre or both. The finishes are applied to;

* Improve the colorfastness to washing
* Improve the colorfastness to crocking
* Improve the colorfastness to light
* Improve the colorfastness to weathering
* Improve the colorfastness to chemicals washes such as mild bleaching, dry cleaning and
* commercial washing.

Resin finishing

Resins are the chemical group used in many of the finishes. Resins are the most widely used chemicals in the textile industry. They are used for many purposes, primarily on cellulosic and cellulosic blend fabrics. Resins have a profound effect on and cause changes in the hand (feel), drapability and physical characteristics of textiles. While many benefits are achieved through these changes, there are also some Short Comings. Resins modify fabrics in the following ways:

* They add stiffness to fabrics and are thus used as stiffening agents or to create a firm hand.
* Resins stabilize fabrics in the same shape or configuration as when the resin was cured. Fabrics cured m a smooth, non-wrinkled condition will return to that shape after being wrinkled in wear, while fabrics cured with creases in garments will retain these creases.
* Yarns in fabric will be stabilized and will resist shrinkage in laundering. Fabrics will become less moisture absorbent, thus drying more rapidly. They will also be less comfortable in warm, humid weather.
* Most resins produce an offensive "fish-like" or formaldehyde odour in fabric. This odour eventually disappears on exposure to air and/or laundering.
* Resins combine chemically with cellulosic fibres (cotton, rayon,*etc.*) to cause significant reductions in abrasion resistance, breaking strength and tear strength. This reduction can be as high as 50%.
* Resins have an affinity for oily soils, creating a soiling problem. Soil release finishes help alleviate this objection.

Plasma finish

Plasma treatment is a surface modifying process, where a gas (air, oxygen, nitrogen, argon,carbon dioxide and so on), injected inside a reactor at a pressure of approximately 0.5 mbar, is ionised by the presence of two electrodes between which is a high-frequency electric field. The need to create the vacuum is justified by the necessity to obtain a so-called cold plasma with a temperature no higher than 80 °C. This, with the same energy content that can be reached at atmospheric pressure at a temperature of some thousands of degrees Celsius, permits the treatment of fabrics even with a low melting point such as polypropylene and polyethylene, without causing any form of damage.The fabric, sliding through the electrodes, is subject to a true bombardment from the elements that constitute the plasma (ions, electrons, UV radiation and so on) and which come from the decomposition of gas and contain a very high level of kinetic energy. The surface of the fabric exposed to the action of the plasma is modified, both physically (roughness), as well as chemically, to remove organic particles still present and to prepare for the successive introduction of free radicals and new chemical groups inside the molecular chain on the surface of the material. The mechanical properties remain, on the other hand, unaltered, as the treatment is limited to the first molecular layers.

Enzyme Finishing

Bio polishing, and bio-polishing, is a finishing process applied to cellulosic textiles that produces permanent effects by the use of enzymes. Bio-finishing removes protruding fibres and slubs from fabrics, significantly reduces pilling, softens fabric hand and provides a smooth fabric appearance, especially forknitwear and as a pretreatment for printing.

Sewing Thread Finishing

Apart from many of the above said finishes which can be applied to sewing threads also, A variety of finishes are used to improve the sewability of sewing thread,for example

- ❖ Lubricants reduce friction and improve the lubricity of the thread. Lubricity refers to the frictional characteristics of thread as it passes through the sewing machine and into the seam. Good lubricity characteristics will minimize thread breakage and enhance sewability.
- ❖ Glazing increases strength and abrasion resistance. Glaze Finish refers to a finish put on 100% cotton threads or cotton-polyester core spun thread made from starches, waxes or other additives. This coating is then brushed to give the thread a smooth surface. A glaze finish protects the thread during sewing giving better ply security and abrasion resistance.
- ❖ Bonding to increase strength and surface smoothness. Bonded Finish refers to a finish applied to continuous filament nylon and a polyester thread which coats the fibers, giving the thread better ply security and abrasion resistance.

Mechanical Finishing

2

2.1. Introduction

The term finishing includes all the mechanical and chemical processes employed commercially to improve the acceptability of the product, except those procedures directly concerned with colouring. The objective of the various finishing processes is to make fabric from the loom or knitting frame more acceptable to the consumer. Finishing processes include preparatory treatments used before additional treatment. Any operation (other than preparation or dyeing) in the manufacture of textiles to improve the appearance and imparts useful characteristics to the fabric. May gives same basic fabric multiple uses to over market versatility.

2.2. Classification of Textile Finishing

Finishing of textile fabric is carried out to increase attractiveness and serviceability of the fabric. Different finishing treatments are available to get various effects, which add the value to the basic textile material. Value Adding Textile finishes are classified as four types they are;

- **Mechanical finishes**
- **Thermo-Mechanical finishes**
- **Chemical finishes**
- **Special finishes**

Terms Used to Categorize Finishes

- ❖ Chemical finishing
- ❖ Physical (Mechanical) finishing
- ❖ Wet
- ❖ Dry
- ❖ Durable
- ❖ Non-durable
- ❖ Physical finishing

Physical (Mechanical) finishes usually involved specific physical treatment to fabric surface to causes change in fabric appearance. This is also known as dry finish.

Types of Physical Finishing (Mechanical)

- ❖ Heat Setting
- ❖ Raising
- ❖ Milling
- ❖ Sanforising
- ❖ Shearing
- ❖ Calendaring
- ❖ Decatizing
- ❖ Compacting
- ❖ Relaxation Drying

2.2.1   Heat setting

- ❖ Process for stabilizing polyester and nylon fabrics by heating at 350-4000F for 20-60 seconds.
- ❖ Uneven moisture causes the fabric to dry unevenly and therefore be subjected to uneven heat setting.
- ❖ Not effective on cotton or rayon.
- ❖ May be performed in fabric or garment form.
- ❖ Differential dyeing, bow-bias and yellowing can result.
- ❖ May cause shade variation from side-to-side if done prior to dyeing.
- ❖ May cause variations in shrinkage.

2.2.2   Raising

The raising of the fiber on the face of the goods by means of teasels or rollers covered with card clothing (steel wires) that is about one inch in height. Action by either method raises the protruding fibres and causes the finished fabric to prov ide greater warmth to the wearer, makes the cloth more compact, causes the fabric to become softer in hand or smoother in feel. Napped fabrics include blankets, flannel, unfinished worsted, and several types of coatings and some dress goods. Soft and supple handle is one of those efficient tools which had done wonders in elaborating the definitions of value added requirements for fabric. Therefore Raising involves lifting up of fibres to a considerable height so that there may be no disturbance in fabric construction. Machine required for this purpose involves fabric movement over a central drum mounted with series of pile and counter pile rollers having their movement in such a fashion that each fibres in lifted in a controlled manner. This finishing work is used to create different feel & a velvety material surface on fabrics & knitwear by loosening a large number of individual fibres from the fabric & subsequent rising & napping in order to crest a dense raised fabric/surface.

Two main types as follows;

❖ Using wire-covered rolls to "dig out" individual fiber ends to the surface Fabric construction and yarn has big effect on the pile.

❖ Important to have a napping lubricant on the fabric to aid in pile raising.

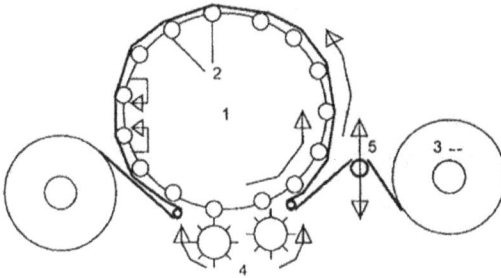

1. roller
2. rollers equipped with hooks
3. fabric
4. nib cleaning brushes
5. fabric tension adjustment

Fig. 2.1: Raising finishing

2.2.3 Calendaring

Calendaring is defined as the modification of the surface of a fabric by the action of heat and pressure. Calendaring is a high speed ironing process that primarily imparts luster and is usually the final treatment for the fabrics in the finishing sequence. The basic principle of calendaring is to expose the cloth to the combined effect of moisture, heat and pressure until the fabric acquires a very smooth and light reflecting surface and gets a good luster The finish is obtained by passing the fabric between heated rotating rollers (Smooth or Engraved) when both speed of rotation and pressure applied are variable. Calendering is a mechanical finishing process used on cloth where fabric is folded in half and passed under rollers at high temperatures and pressures. Calendering is used on fabrics such as moire to produce its watered effect and also on cambric and some types of sateens. . The calendaring effect on the fabric is usually temporary and disappears after first washing. Semi permanent luster is sometimes achieved by padding fabric in a soluble polyvinyl acetate emulsion before calendaring, where the solution acts as a binding agent. More permanent finish can be obtained by treating fabric with a solution of crease recovery reagent, followed by drying, calendaring and curing the fabric at about 150 °C. The calendars are basically an assembly of heavy rolls, alternatively of iron and paper or cotton that are normally mounted in vertical frames. The rolls are bearing one on the other under a high pressure that is applied by compound levers or hydraulic or pneumatic equipment. Textile fabrics are taken through the process of calendering to improve their aesthetic appearance and handle. Calendering is a thermo-mechanical process, i.e. it involves the use of heat and mechanical pressure, but no chemicals.

2.2.3.1 Objective of Calendaring

❖ To improve the fabric handle and to impart a smooth silky touch to the fabric

❖ To compress the fabric and reduce its thickness.

❖ To reduce the air permeability by closing the threads.

❖ To cause a closing together of the threads of the fabric by flattening them and thus tending to fill up the interstices between warp and weft.

❖ To produce a smooth, glossy and highly lustrous appearance on the surface of the cloth.

❖ To reduce air permeability and water permeability of fabric by changing its porosity.

❖ To increase the luster.

❖ To reduce the yarn slippage.

❖ To increase the opacity of the fabric

❖ Surface patterning by embossing

2.2.3.2 Process of calendaring

❖ Fabric is passed between rolls under heavy pressure. Calendaring machine

❖ One roll is usually metal and the other is usually covered with paper or fabric.

❖ The temperature ranges from cold to 500°F, while pressure may range from 200 lbs/in^2 to 2500 lbs / in^2.

❖ Moisture in the form of water or steam may be used to achieve a desired luster.

Key Components of calendaring

❖ Composition of calendar roll

❖ Pressure

❖ Heat

❖ Moisture

2.2.3.3 Fabric Characteristics after calendaring

❖ Becomes thinner, less permeable, has more cover and luster.

❖ Too much pressure makes the fabric papery.

❖ Excessive heat and pressure will cause too much luster.

❖ Scarred surface rolls will imprint the defect onto the fabric.

❖ Effect is usually permanent on thermoplastic fibers.

❖ Resins required to be used to make calendaring durable on cellulosic fabrics. Without the resin the effect lasts only one laundering.

After a grey fabric is subjected to scouring, bleaching, mercerizing etc, it is finally dried to retain its true shape and dimensions. But in this state the fabric becomes least lustrous. Because of those operations the threads in fabric become wavy and crimped. But if a fabric is to appear highly lustrous then its surface should be perfectly flat and fibres appeared on the surface should be parallel to each other and all should lie in the length direction. To fulfill this object cotton, linen, rayon, silk materials are applied a temporary physical finish which is known as calendaring. In this process fabric is passed through a series of heated rollers under pressure in open width form.

In calendering, the threads of the fabric are closed to give it the required gloss (luster) or feel. An ordinary calender consists of a series of hard and soft (resilient) bowls (rollers) placed in a definite order. The soft roller may be compressed cotton or paper. The calender may consist of 3, 5, 6, 7 or 10 rollers. These would respectively be called 3-bowl calender, 5-bowl calender, 6-bowl calender and so on. The sequence of rollers is that no two hard rollers are in contact with each other. The pressure and heat applied in calendaring depends on the type of the finish required. In a typical 7-bowl calender, (e.g. a Farmer-Norton Calender) the arrangement of the bowls is as given in the figure. Generally, the compressible (soft) bowls are made of cotton, wool, linen paper or flax paper. The hard metal bowl is either of chilled iron or close-grained cast iron or steel. Iron bowls are made with a highly polished hard surface and are heated from inside by steam or gas and provide the gloss to the calendared fabric. Calendars with more than three bowls can be used as swissing, chasing or friction calendars, to produce different effects on the fabric. Such calendars are called universal calendars.

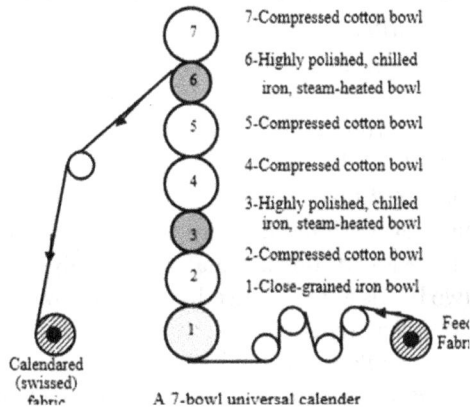

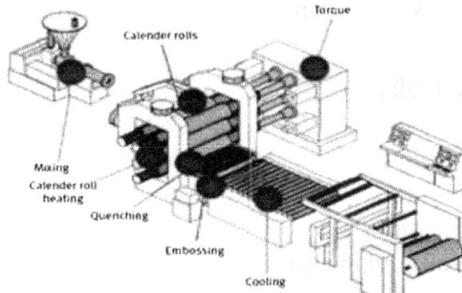

7-Compressed cotton bowl
6-Highly polished, chilled iron, steam-heated bowl
5-Compressed cotton bowl
4-Compressed cotton bowl
3-Highly polished, chilled iron, steam-heated bowl
2-Compressed cotton bowl
1-Close-grained iron bowl

Feed Fabric

Calendared (swissed) fabric

A 7-bowl universal calender

Fig. 2.2: Calendaring fabric

Paper or cotton rolls are made by compressing sheets of paper and cotton under heavy pressure of hundreds of tons and then finely turned to produce a smooth surface. The iron rolls are also called chilled rolls because these are hardened by sudden chilling of the red-hot rolls. These are hollow so as to allow passage of steam or sometimes gas-fire to heat these to different temperatures. The calendaring effect produced depends upon the following factors.

i. Moisture content in the fabric

ii. The number of bowls of the calender used

iii. The composition of the bowls (steel-cotton, cotton-cotton, steel-paper, cotton-plastic, *etc.*)

iv. Arrangement of bowls

v. Temperature

vi. Pressure

vii. Fabric speed

2.2.3.4 Types of calendaring

❖ Friction calendaring

❖ Schreiner calendaring

❖ Embossing calendaring

❖ Swissing or normal gloss or simple calendaring

❖ Cire calendaring

2.2.3.5 Friction Calendaring

The friction-calendaring operation produces a high degree of lustre on one side of the fabric (this is the side that touches the iron bowl); it also results in the closing up of the interlacing threads. For producing this effect, the top four bowls of a 7-bowl universal calender are lifted up, disengaging or disconnecting the contact between the third and the fourth bowls, so as to use only the two or three bottom bowls. When the first two bowls alone are used, the arrangement is a two-bowl friction calender and if the first three are used it is a three-bowl friction calender. The latter arrangement is shown in the figure below. In this process, the third (top), polished, chilled iron bowl is heated with steam. As a further modification, this bowl is rotated by means of special gear wheels such that its surface speed is double that of the fabric and those of the lower two bowls.

❖ Usually 3 roll process

❖ B central cotton fabric or paper roll is sandwiched between two metal rolls which are turned at very fast speeds as compared to the cotton roll.

❖ The fabric to be calendared is laced between the metal rolls and the cotton roll, and the surface of this cloth is brought to a highly polished state.

❖ Starches and waxes give a temporary glaze, while durable glazes are generated from fabrics treated with resins.

As a variation, the top bowl may be run at 1½ times the speed of the lowest bowl, with the middle bowl running at an intermediate speed. Due to the differential bowl speeds, a frictional effect is exerted on the fabric surface. Fabrics are generally given a starch finish before calendering. The starch content and moisture in the fabric affects the calendering. If the moisture content in the fabric is more than 20%, the starch sticks to the calender bowls and if it is less than 15%, sufficient lustre is not produced and the fabric acquires a hard feel. The final effect in friction calendering is quite similar to that seen and felt in an ironed garment.

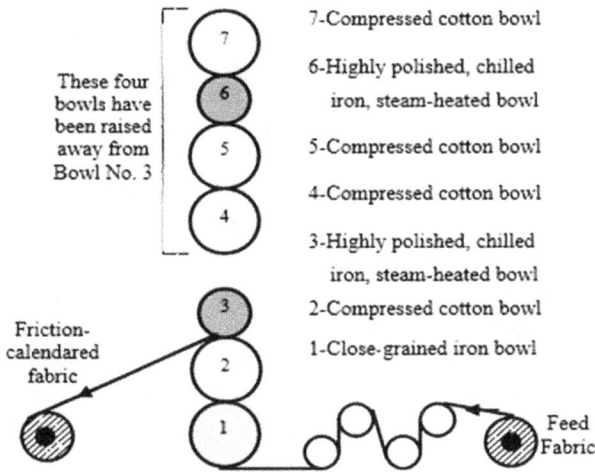

A 7-bowl universal calender modified and used as
3-bowl friction calendar

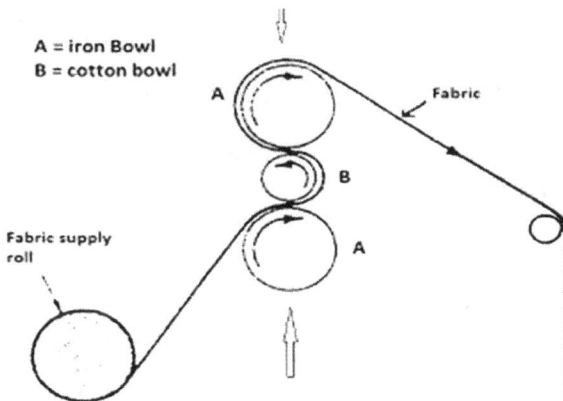

Fig. 2.3: Friction calendaring

A 3-bowl friction calender is generally run at about 30 m/min. A three-bowl calender, working without friction is run at around 60 m/min, while a seven–bowl calender is run around 80 m/min; the actual speed is determined by the kind of finish desired on the fabric and by the number of bowls used. When a light finish is required higher speeds than those mentioned above may be selected. Some seven-bowl calenders are run at speeds of 130-230 m/min.

2.2.3.6 Schreinering

The schreiner finish can be imparted to textile fabric by means of a schreiner calender. This operation gives a silk-like brilliance to cotton fabric. This is carried out chiefly on cotton linings, sateen and printed fabrics. When produced on mercerised fabric it gives the nearest possible resemblance to silk. The silk-like finish is due to the fine lines (5-20/mm) engraved on the steel roller of the schreiner calender. A large number of lines are thus embossed on the cloth that is passed through the calender. The engraving is so cut on the steel roll of the calender that the lines are at a small angle with respect to the directions of the warp and weft threads in the fabric. In weft sateen, the best finishes are obtained with the lines at an angle of about 20° to the weft and in the direction of the twist. Ordinary plain weave cotton fabric is also greatly improved in appearance and handle by a schreiner finish; in this case, the calender has a steel roller with coarse lines (6-7 mm) engraved on it. A typical schreiner calender has strong frames carrying two bowls 7.5 cm (in diameter), the top one being made of special, fine-grained steel; it is engraved with the required number of lines and is gas-heated from the inside. The bearings of this bowl are cooled by water. The upper roller is in contact with the lower cotton bowl when the machine is running and is separated while not in use in order to keep the cotton bowl from any damage. The top bowl is fixed while the lower one is moved up or down. The required pressure is exerted by hydraulic rams positioned underneath the bearing of the bottom bowl. Very high pressure is exerted on the fabric while it passes through the nip. The calender is provided with a relief valve allowing the bowls to be separated instantly. Skewing arrangement is provided for the bearing of the lower bowl by which it can be set at any angle to the top roll. An enhanced brilliance can be obtained by using the skewing arrangement. A typical 2-roll schreiner calender has 325-cm wide rolls, which can exert a pressure of up to 140 tonnes.

❖ Large metal roll engraved at a 260 angle with fine lines (250-300/in.) presses on the fabric surface.

❖ Result is a soft, silk-like luster on cotton and linen. Soft, opaque lingerie fabrics are produced from tricot knits by Schreinering.

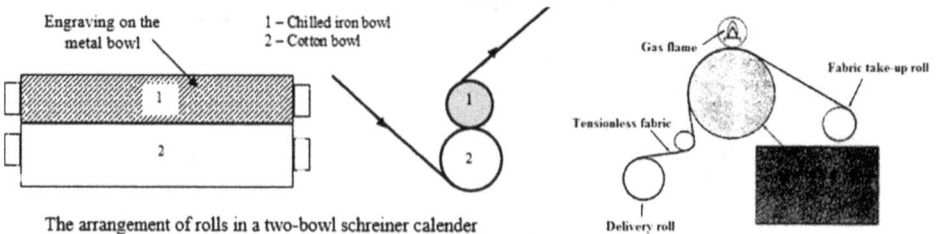

The arrangement of rolls in a two-bowl schreiner calender

Fig. 2.4: Schreiner calendaring

2.2.3.7 Embossing

Embossing is a particular calendaring process through which a simple pattern can be engraved on the cloth. The machine is made up of a heated and embossed roller made of steel, which is pressed against another roller coated with paper or cotton, its circumference being exactly a whole multiple of the metal roller. A gear system drives the harmonized motion of the roller. A gear system drives s the harmonized motion of the rollers, preventing them from sliding and granting a sharp engraving of the patterned design. After being engraved, the pattern can be stabilized by means of an appropriate high-temperature treatment or by applying suitable starchy substances. The process can be applied of fabrics made of all types of fibres with the exception of wool. This finish is pretreatment when applied to fabrics made of thermoplastic fibres. It is not permanent when applied to untreated fabrics made of natural fibres or man-made fibres that are not thermoplastic. However, if these fabrics are treated with certain chemical resins, the embossing is considered to be pretreatment.

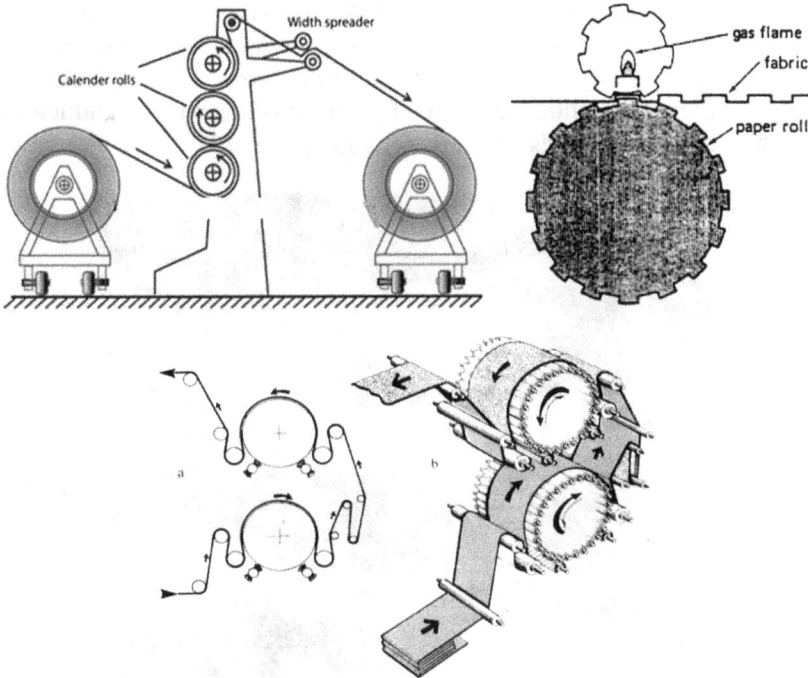

Fig. 2.5: Embossing Rolls for raised designs

To preserve the embossed finish of such fabrics, they should be washed in lukewarm water with a mild soap, never be bleached, and be ironed on the wrong side while damp.

- ❖ Usually a two roll special calendar.
- ❖ Uses a heated metal roll with an engraved pattern surface and a paper roll with the negative of the pattern on the metal or without a pattern.
- ❖ Fabric is passed between these rolls and the pattern is set into the fabric by heat and pressure. Thermoplastic fibers can be set by heat.
- ❖ Cotton fabrics must have a resin finish to give a durable effect.

Advantages

❖ Crepes or pebble effect may be produced.

❖ Temporary and permanent effect may be produced by different of pressure and heat.

❖ Due to smaller metallic bowl, cost is less.

❖ Generally used for synthetic fabrics. It cannot create any effect on cotton fabric.

2.2.3.8 Swizzing effect

Swissing means running the cloth through all the nips of a 10-bowl universal calender and then either plaiting or batching the fabric; the threading of the fabric is the same as shown in the fig. 2.6. This operation closes the interstices (the spaces in between the interlacing threads) in the cloth and gives it a smooth appearance. A 10-bowl calender used for swissing gives a very large production. Prior to calendering, a softening and filling agent should be applied (as the finishing mix) to produce lustrous fabric. In swissing, all the bowls rotate at the same speed.

Fig. 2.6

In this operation, if a cold calender is used, moderate smoothness and a regular surface lustre of the fabric are produced. A hot calender, where the metal bowls are heated by steam or gas from the inside, produces greater smoothness and a more lustrous fabric surface. When all the bowls of a universal calender are used, the fabric acquires a smooth appearance and gloss without the high glaze that is so characteristic of a friction calendered fabric.

2.2.3.9 Chasing calender

In a chasing calender, the cotton fabric passes normally through the nips of a 7-bowl calender, then over the *chasing* rollers. The cloth is then fed again into the cotton nip of the calender so that it is led back into the machine. This is repeated several times, such that each layer of cloth lies one over another. This is shown in the figure that follows. Chasing gives the cloth a thready-linen appearance and a special handle.

2.3.3.10 Chasing calender with water mangle

In a variation, a water mangle precedes the calender and the mangled fabric is passed through the calender a number of times, as explained above, and finally either batched or plaited, as shown in the figure at the right. Roll No. 3 (from the bottom) is the power-driven roll. The alternate rolls (1, 3 and 5) are generally geared together to prevent slipping.

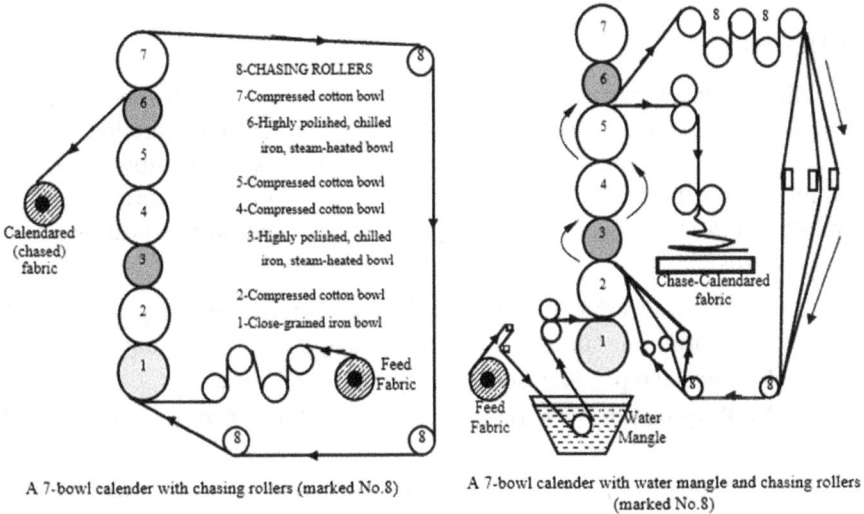

A 7-bowl calender with chasing rollers (marked No.8)

A 7-bowl calender with water mangle and chasing rollers (marked No.8)

Fig. 2.7

When a fabric is water-mangled under high pressure, the threads are well flattened and the spaces between them are closed; if this fabric is taken for starch finishing in a starch mangle, a flat, bonded structure and a better starched finish is obtained with a lower number of starch mangle runs.

2.2.3.11 Felt Calender

Felt calenders are mainly used for imparting lustre and smoothness to silk, rayon and cotton knitwear materials. These work at low pressure and temperature than used for cotton. The cloth is pressed between an endless felt blanket and a hot steel cylinder at a speed of 20 to 40 meters/minutes. By adjusting speeds of the feed and take up rollers the tubular knitwear can be compacted to some extent on this calender.

2.2.3.12 Nipco-Flex Calender

The pressure application concept of this calender is different from the conventional calendering system. The pressing roller consists of a rotating shell that is covered with a highly elastic plastic material named as RACOLAN. The roller has fixed axels on which hydrostatic support elements are mounted that press the racolan shell against either steel or a cotton/paper roller. The hydrostatic pressure is applied with oil and is adjustable according to width of the cloth. The NIPCO roller can be arranged in vertical position or in L shape with a hot steel roller at top and a cotton bowl in front of it.

The main advantages of NIPCO calendar over a conventional calendar are;

- ❖ Attainment of very high pressure.
- ❖ Adjustment of pressure line according to width of cloth.
- ❖ No over load at the fabric selvedge.
- ❖ Easy installation and removal of the rollers.

2.2.3.13 Sueding

This process is carried out by means of a roller coated with abrasive material. Sueding is a mechanical finishing process in which a fabric is abraded on one or both sides to raise or create a fibrous surface. This fibrous surface improves the fabric appearance, gives the fabric a softer, fuller hand, and can mask fabric construction and subdue coloration. Special type of raised surface fabric is corduroy Sueding, sanding- creates softer hand of fabric.

- ❖ Using abrasive-covered rolls (sandpaper, emery cloth, *etc.*) to produce shorter pile surface - does cause an apparent shade change
- ❖ Special type of raised surface fabric is corduroy.
- ❖ Purpose is to cut surface fibers and produce a fuzz, a suede-like surface on the fabric.
- ❖ Fabric is abraded with sandpaper covered rolls (emery cloth, *etc.*)
- ❖ Course paper gives heavier pile whereas fine grit papergives a light pile.

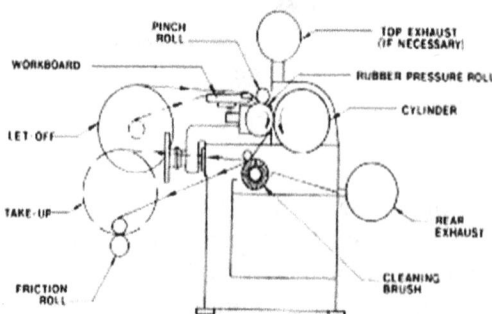

Fig. 2.8: Sueding finishing

Types of Machines

1. Large single roll
2. Series of smaller diameter rolls

Variables

a. Grit of sandpaper
b. Speed of the fabric
c. Speed of the sanding roll
d. Pressure of the sandpaper on the cloth
e. Number and direction of passes through process

Problems are Caused by

a. Folds and creases which give obvious defects.
b. Too much softener loads up sandpaper. Causes shiny appearance.
c. Slubs, knots and heavy selvages cause holes in the fabric.
d. Paper needs to be changed at the proper time to give a uniform product.
e. Multirole machine allows for continuous replacement of roll covers over a preprogrammed schedule.

2.2.4 Compacting

Durable finish imparted on man-made fibres and knitted fabrics by employing heat and pressure to shrink them to produce a crêpey and bulky texture.

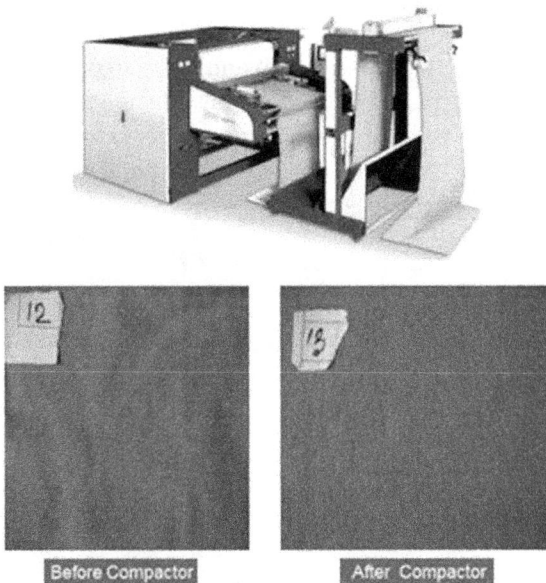

Fig. 2.9: Compacting fabric

2.2.4.1 Sanforizing or Pre Shrinking:

Sanforizing is a process whereby the fabric is run through a sanforizer; a machine that has drums filled with hot steam. This process is done to control the shrinkage of the fabric. The fabric is given an optimum dimensional stability by applying mechanic forces and water vapour.

Fig.2.10: Sanforizing machine

2.2.4.2 Stentering Machine:

A machine or apparatus for stretching or stentering fabrics. The purpose of the stenter machine is to bringing the length and width to pre determine dimensions and also for heat setting and it is used for applying finishing chemicals and also shade variation is adjusted. The main function of the stenter is to stretch the fabric width wise and to recover the uniform width.

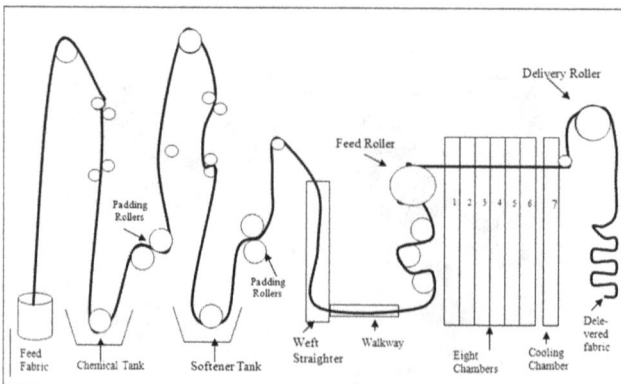

Fig. 2.11: Stentering machine

Functions of Stenter Machines

1. Heat setting is done by the stenter for lycra fabric, synthetic and blended fabric.
2. Width of the fabric is controlled by the stenter.
3. Finishing chemical apply on fabric by the stenter.

2.2.4.3 Tubular compactor

The treatment of knit fabrics in tubular form on the TUBULAR COMPACTOR meets the exacting standards set by customers

Main Machine Parts:

- ❖ Feed section: Tension control & Metal detector.
- ❖ Shape: Set according to the dia. of fabric
- ❖ Steam zone
- ❖ Take out & Plaiter zone
- ❖ Compacting Zone: It's a roller & shoe arrangement & the most important zone which consists of two rollers, the Feed roller (Recarter roller) & the Retard roller. They are heated by Shoe, into which hot thermo-oil runs through.

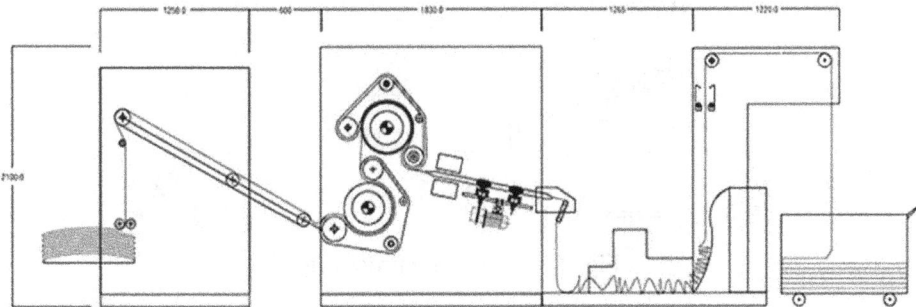

Fig. 2.12: Tube compacting machine

Basic functions of the Tube compactor machine:

- ❖ To control the GSM. (Increase & decrease).
- ❖ To control the dia.
- ❖ To control the shrinkage. (Increase & decrease).
- ❖ Width control through a stepless adjustable special tubular fabric spreader driven by variable speed motor for distortion-free fabric guidance.
- ❖ Steamping with a condensate-free steam box which is easily operated and completely made from stainless stell.
- ❖ Compacting through two Nomex felt belts.
- ❖ Calendaring while passing between the felt belt and the heated shrinking rollers.

2.2.5 Shearing

Shearing is an important preparatory stage in the processing of cotton cloth. The objective of "Shearing" is to remove fibers and loose threads from the surface of the fabric, thus improving surface finish.

❖ Napped fabrics may be sheared to give a fabric of uniform height and even pile.

❖ Smooth fabrics may be sheared to make smoother fabric.

❖ Pilling of some fabrics may be improved by shearing.

❖ Hi-Lo patterns can be created by going over a solid bar. Random patterns are created by using rubber blankets.

❖ Shearing defects are caused by folds creases and heavy edges.

❖ Misaligned blades cause uneven shearing.

❖ Sewn seams must be jumped otherwise the shearer will destroy the seam and damage the blades.

❖ Foreign metallic objects will damage the blades.

❖ Use of rotary blade(s) to trim raised surfaces, primarily napped fabrics, to a uniform height.

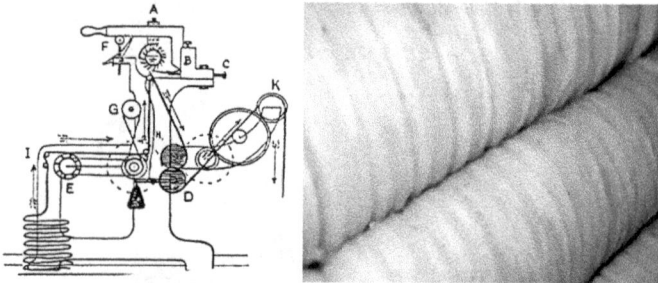

Fig. 2.13: Shearing finishing

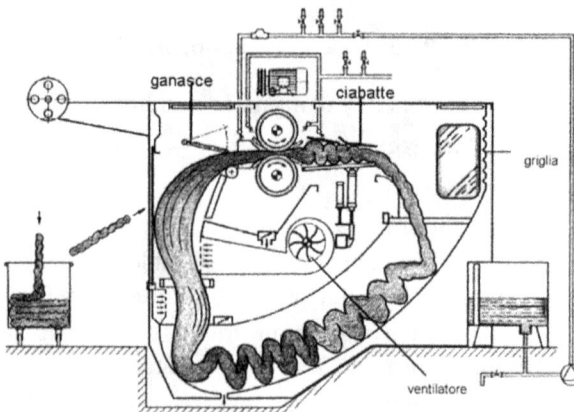

Fig. 2.14: Milling Machines

* ❖ This reduces the tendency of the fabric surface to mat and also reduces the pilling tendency.
* ❖ Special types of blades and conveyor belts can produce pattern effects on the surface.

2.3. Developments in Mechanical Finishes

Mechanical finishes imparts various properties to the fabric such as softness, peach skin effect, luster, bulkiness. In this respect various machines producing special finishes have been introduced by various manufacturing companies such as biancalani, santex, alliace.

2.3.1. Petra From Bianclani (Italy)/ Airo Finish

This is a continuous, modular, open width finishing machine for all types of woven fabrics; it produces smooth and peach skin type finish, enhancing hand and volume through oscillating action of bars of abrasive stone. The oscillating motion of the abrasive bars at a very high frequency against the surface of the fabric causes micro-fibrillation, techno-polishing and/or discoloring of the fabric without any affecting the strength of the fabric or cutting it. This mechanical finish is a alternate to the enzyme finish but is faster and without fabric strength loss. Different looks such as classic look and casual look can be produced by adjustment of the movements and severity of the bars through varying pressure of contrast cylinders mounted below the bars. This machine consists of re-circulation system for water conservation, the user friendly control panel with computerized touch screen system with manual or automatic modes, which can control the fabric speed, pressure of contrast cylinders, depth of abrasion, re-circulation *etc.* The various special finishes such as discoloring effect on the denim fabric, smoothing, peach skin effect surface ageing on the cotton, viscose, lyocell, linen fabric can be produced.

2.3.2. Santasoft from Santex Peach Finish

This machine gives high-grade finish in open width form on woven & knitted. It increases the softness and suppleness of the fabric. The fabric passes through a treatment zone in which the fabric is subjected to intensive tumbling action. It produces excellent finishes on the denims, cotton cord, pigment printed fabrics, linen and blends.

Phantim

This is supposed to be one of the novel effects which are present in the market to have value addition on to the fabric. In real terms it is practiced only on to the denim this is because one of the un-dyed and consequently results in considerable fading of colour due to extensive abrasion. Machine which is used for this purpose involves diamond powder coated roller which results in the required degree of abrasion sufficient enough to fade the colour. Predetermined or desired design could be procured with the help of pneumatically operated needle shape nodes when in contact with the diamond powder coated roller results in fading of that portion. And movement of nodes as well as rotation of the diamond powder coated roller is controlled with the help of computer which creates the design finish meticulously with great precision & accuracy.

2.4 Thermo-Mechanical Finish

This method of giving finishing to the fabric employs application of heat with regular mechanical forces to reduce novel finishes. This finishes include the following;

2.4.1 Calendaring

Calendering belongs to thermo-mechanical type of finish. Though this one of the old types of finishing method yet it holds sheer importance in finishing department. Here fabric is passed in an open width form over a series of consecutively roller placed vertically in such a manner that considerable amount of tension is provided to the fabric. Rollers over which fabric is placed is incorporated with steam which results in improving lustre of fabric after calendaring.

2.4.2 Crush Finish

This is today's most accepted form of finish by young generation especially in case of ladies wear like tops, dupattas and shirts. This finish can be obtained by incorporating high twisted yarn during weaving. The finish can also be obtained in cotton blends, where POY (partially oriented yarn) is used along with cotton.

2.4.3 Embossing

This type of finishing is only demanded for designer wear. It could be designed with the help of two rollers out of which one roller being male having non designed part carved & other being female made up of either cotton or paper. During the course of passing fabric pressure which is applied by the male roller over female leads in engraving of the design. Application of design becomes stronger with sufficient amount of heat, which results in exquisite results on the fabric & contributes in enhancing value of the fabric.

2.4.4 Pinching

Machine which is used for pinching involves a die which can be simplified into a steel streaked model to press out stress & is able to change streaks very rapidly. By running this steel streaked model and altering various functions of the computer, variety types of streaks can be ignored. With the help of these types of machines designer streaks can be performed easily on synthetic fibres clothing apart from that it also used in tailored pattern in scarves, women clothing *etc.*

2.4.5 Pleating

This type of finish can be applied to procure pleating on to the fabric with the help of knives and rollers various pleating effects could be derived by altering the types of knives and rollers. Apart from types of pleat, sequences, extent of different pleats and length of group and space pleats could be computer designed to get unlimited pleat variation. Here the finish mainly involves creation of very varied shapes & arrangements of folds on textiles using various machines. The term pleat comes from the French, and is used to describe material pressed into narrow folds. Various types of pleating machines fare involved as follows,

- ❖ Knife, squeezing & group pleating machine for the generation of wide range of patterns (less than 1mm)
- ❖ Crystal pleating machines for the generation of vertical folds. (1-5mm fold height)
- ❖ Accordion pleating machine for upstanding folds. (5-50mm)

3 Functional Finishes

3.1. Wrinkle free finish

Resin or wrinkle free finishing is widely used in the textile industry to impart wrinkle-resistance to cotton fabrics and garments. Considerable loss in strength and abrasion resistance of the finished fabrics has been a major concern for the industry. Enhancing dimensional stability and wrinkle resistance with resin finishing of cotton has constantly been correlated with lower abrasion resistance and tear strength. The strength of the fibre depends on how much the cross-linked chains can still be mutually displaced under tension in order to sufficiently resist the applied load. The rigid cross-links that are formed with the DMDHEU obviously prevent the redistribution of stress by preventing movement within the fibre microstructure. The cross-linking of cellulose molecules with these relatively rigid cross-links causes stiffening of the cellulosic macromolecular network and fibre embitterment, thus dropping the mechanical strength of the treated cotton fabrics. These same mechanisms are responsible for reduced mechanical properties of the fibre surface, thus leading to strength loss. Fibre surface property alteration, such as through the use of softeners, has been shown to play an important task in minimizing strength loss.

Recent health risk assessment of the possible effects of continued exposure to formaldehyde vapour to humans has increased the desirability of finding durable press reagents, which do not release formaldehyde. Such cellulose cross-linking agents must meet a number of stringent requirements to be considered for practical use in crease proof or Durable Press (DP) finishing. Many classes of chemical compounds have been investigated as replacement for formaldehyde emitting cross-linking agents based on dimethylol dihidroxy ethylene urea (DMDHEU), which are still the most widely used finishing agents. Majority of the Poly- carboxylic acids (PCA) give satisfactory results of DP performance and wrinkle recovery angle. The creasing behavior of cotton fabric is directly related to the free hydroxyl groups present in the amorphous regions, which are bound to each other. To impart crease resistance finish to the cotton material, the hydrogen bond formation of the hydroxyl groups should be either masked or totally removed. A popular and widely used method of imparting the crease resistant finish is the one in which the hydroxyl groups of adjacent macro molecules are reacted with bi-functional chemicals forming a cross-link with elimination of water or methanol molecules.

❖ Formaldehyde has many advantages as a cross-linking agent, including low chemical cost and high finish durability, whereas this process is notorious for lack of control, high strength loss of treated cotton and release of excessive fumes in the atmosphere. It was found that formaldehyde and hydrochloric acid in the presence of water can form Bichloromethyl ether (BCME), which is human carcinogen, irritant and causes allergy to human beings. Citric acid has been identified as a successful non-formaldehyde based cross-linking agent.

❖ PCA which react readily with cotton at an elevated temperature, Citric acid has showed higher reactivity when applied to cotton in the same way.

❖ One of the aim is to combine ecological with economical demands, which we have tried to accomplish with the application of cheaper PCA – Citric acid. Citric acid mixed with Trisodiumcitrate in different ratios to obtain similarly good crease-proof effects as with the DMDHEU.

❖ The mixture of inadequate scratch resistance and relatively severe tensile and tear strength loss has been a major disadvantage for resin finished 100% cotton fabrics. The objectives of this work are to investigate the cause and mechanism of loss in abrasion resistance of cross linked cotton fabrics; relationships between the molecular structure of cross-linking agents and their effect on the mechanical properties of cross-linked textile structures; and develop a technology for improving the tear strength of resin finished cotton fabrics by adding special silicones.

3.1.1. Types of Wrinkle Free Process of Cotton Shirts

Cellulosic fiber-containing fabrics are made wrinkle resistant by a durable press wrinkle-free process which comprises treating a cellulosic fiber-containing fabric with formaldehyde, a catalyst capable of catalyzing the crosslinking reaction between the formaldehyde and cellulose and a silicone elastomer, heat-curing the treated cellulose fiber-containing fabric, preferably having a moisture content of more than 20% by weight, under conditions at which formaldehyde reacts with cellulose in the presence of the catalyst without a substantial loss of formaldehyde before the reaction of the formaldehyde with cellulose to improve the wrinkle resistance of the fabric in the presence of a silicone elastomeric softener to provide higher wrinkle resistance, and better tear strength after washing, with less treatment.

The idea of a shirt which has not to be ironed anymore is as old as the cotton shirt itself. Apart from all attempts which has started decades ago to establish a shirt of Polyester or any other artificial fibre failed, as the consumer understood from the beginning the positive attributes of the cotton fibre. By its ability to hold moisture and to release it controlled, cotton is one of the most ideal fibres among all. It is breathable and remains a good feeling for the garment bearer. This may has changed by today's new developments of artificial fibres, which have nothing to do with those from the sixties of the last century. But still the cotton fibre is number one in peoples mind when they think of comfort. In the last decade new technologies have been established to prepare the cotton fabric by chemicals, to make them almost wrinkle free or, as some manufacturer call it wrinkle resistant (WR). Basically four different technologies are known today to do so.

- ❖ Pre- Curing
- ❖ Post- Curing
- ❖ Dip- Spin
- ❖ Vapor – Phase

3.1.2. Pre- Cured fabric

Fabric can be a 100 % cotton fabric or cotton blend. Contrary to all the other WR processes, by this system the fabric does not need any further heat treatment as the curing process has been done already before the shirt is manufactured. The already finished fabric is resistant to wrinkles already. Unfortunately no crisp and sharp creases can be realist for collars, cuffs and front placket edges. As the fabric does not accept any final pressing. Only a shirt finisher with steam and air is required.

3.1.3. Post- Cured fabric

In this case the fabric can be a 100 % cotton fabric or a cotton blend. The fabric will be delivered with the curing chemical inside. The roll of fabric is sealed in a polyester bag . Once the bag is opened the fabric has to be manufactured entirely, as it cannot be stored for a long time. After the shirt is manufactured, it has to be pressed entirely. After it has been put on a hanger it will be cured in a hanging position on a cloth rack inside an oven for 3- 5 min. by about 130°C to 150°C (depends on the chemical used). Now the shirt is ready for folding and bagging.

3.1.4. Dip- Spin system

This one belongs to the most popular process for wrinkle free shirts and can be used for 100 % cotton fabrics or cotton blends. After the shirt is manufactured as usually, it will be dipped into a mixture of chemicals, which will be absorbed by the cotton fibres. After the treatment in a tumbler the shirt is still moisturized and has to be pressed entirely. Important is, that during the pressing operation on the various Veit- Kannegiesser Collar-, Cuff- and Body- Presses, the curing process will start already. After pressing the shirt will be put on a hanger and can be cured in a curing oven by about 140°C for about 3 -5 min. One of the key factors for a perfect appearance is the pressing quality, as after the curing operation in an oven, all wrinkles will stay for life. A re-touching by an iron is impossible.

3.1.5. Vapor – Phase

This curing system can be used in some countries only as very aggressive chemicals are used. Similar to the DIP SPIN system the shirt is manufactured as usually. After the final pressing, a special curing oven is used as instead of liquid chemicals, gas is used to make the shirt resistant to wrinkles. The gas is circulating through the oven and penetrates into the cotton fibre. After a while the gas has to be evacuated from the oven. Before the shirt is folded and bagged, it needs to be washed in order to remove left chemicals inside.

3.1.6. Tear and Tensile Resistance

An overwhelming majority of durable press finishing agents used today are formaldehyde based reagents, such as dimethyloldihydroxyethyleneurea (DMDHEU) and modified DMDHEU, with magnesium chloride as a catalyst.

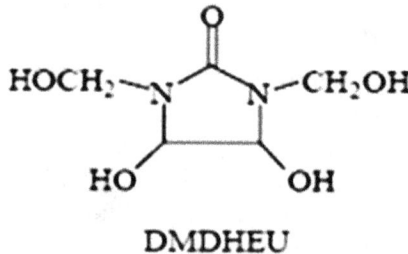

$$\text{HOCH}_2-\underset{\text{HO}}{\text{N}}\overset{\text{O}}{\underset{}{\diagup\!\!\diagdown}}\underset{\text{OH}}{\text{N}}-\text{CH}_2\text{OH}$$

DMDHEU

The following summarizes some of the important aspects so far:

4. The catalysts used for DMDHEU systems, such as magnesium chloride, cause degradation of cellulose, thus reducing the tensile and tear strength of cotton fabric. The magnitude of fabric strength loss is affected by temperature, time, and concentration of the catalyst. Fabric strength loss also depends on both the cation and anion of the catalyst. An activated catalyst system, which includes an organic acid, causes more severe fabric tensile strength loss.

5. Tensile strength loss of cotton fabric treated with DMDHEU is due to both the cross-linking of cellulose and the degradation of cellulose caused by the catalyst. Because a catalyst system plays such an important role in influencing the strength loss of cotton fabrics cross-linked by DMDHEU, the selection of the catalyst system and its concentration is crucial for optimizing the tensile strength retention of the finished fabrics.

6. DMDHEU can be removed from the finished fabric by using an alkali treatment, as evidenced by the decrease in wrinkle recovery angle with removal. The fabric strength gradually increases as the hydrolysis of the cross-linked fabric progresses, indicating that the fabric strength loss due to cross-linking the cellulose molecules is reversible and that it can be restored by removing the cross-links. The remainder of the

strength loss, which has been described as being due to acid-induced de-polymerization, is permanent and is not reversible upon hydrolysis of the cross-links.

3.2. Water Repellent finish

Finishes that repel water, oil, and dry dirt are important in all parts of the textiles market for clothing, home and technical textiles. Water repellency is achieved using different products groups, but oil repellency is attained only by fluorocarbon polymers. The oldest repellent finish is to repel water. Aim of finish is that drops of water should not spread on the surface of the textiles and should not wet the fabric, wetting occur when in form of droplet is absorbed by fabric. Most finishing it is desirable that drops stay on the surface and easily drips off or can be brushed off. The drops should stay on the surface and easily drips off. Similarly, oil repellent finishes should prevent oily fluids from wetting treated textiles. In a similar manner, soil repellent finishes should protect textiles from both dry and wet soils. In all cases, the air permeability of the finished fabric should not be significantly reduced. Water repellency maintains air permeability or breath ability of fabric and is not significantly reduced. In Water proof, breathable water droplets should not penetrate into fabric but perspiration should. To create a surface with low surface energy, so that the interaction between surface and fluid is less than internal between fluids and fluids, therefore a fluid drops off. Water proofing is a finishing that would withstand the hydrostatic pressure exerted by a column of water 1 m in a depth before the first drop is able to penetrate inside. Water proof extreme form of water repellency swim costume but they are extremely stiff handle and lack of air and vapor permeability and hence discomfort to the wearer. Water proof breathable and coating with micro pores. Size is too small for water droplets to penetrate but pores were large enough for perspiration vapors to escape. In addition to the desired repellence effects, other undesirable fabric properties are often found with repellent finishes. These include problems with static electricity, poor soil removal in aqueous laundering stiffer fabric hand, graying (soil redeposition) during aqueous laundering, and increased flammability. Some fabric properties that are often improved by improved by repellent finishes include better durable press properties, more rapid drying and ironing, and increased resistance to acids, bases and other chemicals.

3.2.1. Developments in water repellents

1. Wax dispersions free of metal ions
2. Metallic salts and soaps
3. Wax dispersions containing Zirconium salts and Pyrdinium compounds.
4. Silicones
5. Organo Chronium compounds
6. Flurochemicals.

Products falling under 1 to 4 categories were purely temporary and lasted only a few washes. This led to the development of Silicone compounds. Methyl

Hydrogen Polysiloxane (MeSIOH) was a very popular waterrepellent finish and had lot of risks associated with it. MeSIOH are reactive in nature and great care had to be taken while handling these materials. These materials came in many forms such as fluids, emulsions and resins. SIH products evolve hydrogen upon contact with strong bases, amines, primary alcohols. SIH compounds rapidly evolve hydrogen gas and form flammable and explosive mixtures in air. The inherent risk involved with these compounds made them unpopular and unattractive for waterrepellent finishing operations. More over compounds based on Parrafin oil with Silicone waterrepellent finishing agents were not sufficient to protect textiles from grease and oil stains. This led to the development of FLURO CARBON POLYMERS. (FCP) Cellulosic fibers, wool and silk are prone to stain faster than synthetic fibers because of their hydrophilic nature.

Natural fibers exhibit little or no water repellency, but when they get soiled they are readily cleaned, thus exhibiting a high degree of soil releasability many synthetic fibers notably polyester exhibit a low level of soil releasability. Thus the trend of producing textiles having a natural and synthetic blend of fibers tends to aggravate the situation, because these blends are easily soiled and the absorbed soil is difficult to wash out. Fluorocarbon polymers are applied to textiles in an attempt to solve this problem, however, they make soil release properties worse, because the aqueous washing medium cannot wet the substrate and hence cannot remove the stain, conversely, the addition of hydrophilic soil release polymers tends to enhance the soil release characteristics, but limits the ability of the textile to resist and repel water and oil based liquids.

3.2.2. Fluorocarbon polymers and its chemistry

Chemically fluorocarbon polymers, also known as Perfluroalkylacrylate copolymer and its fundamental structure resemble acrylic resins. Fluorocarbon polymers are special class of polymers and represent an indispensable part of the technology of water and oilrepellent finishing and contain Carbon and Fluorine bonds. The relatively low reactivity and high polarity of the carbon- fluorine imparts unique characteristics to fluorocarbon polymers. FCP decreases the wettability but form waterrepellent and oilrepellent polymer on its surface. A fluropolymer sheth around the fibers strongly reduces the textiles surface free energy, accompanied by the increase of the contact angle of liquids on its surface.

FCP are applied by the normal pad dry- cure technique, where in the substrate align the fluorocarbon segments of the polymers, there by reducing the tendency of soil, oil and water to adhere to the fibers of the substrates. Fluorocarbon polymers typically include a fluorinated component and a non fluorinated polymeric back bone. The fluorinated part called the Perfluoroalkyl group is common to all fluorochemical protectors. Greater the number of fluorine atoms attached to the carbon atoms and the more closely packed, they are, the better the water repellency. It has also been determined that the optimal number of linking carbon atoms is between 10 and 12. Linked carbon atoms that are linear rather than branched give better performance.

The non fluorinated part, in addition to being an extender by lowering the cost of the fluorochemical, serves two other useful purposes. It forms a backbone to the flurochemical making it more durable and acts as a glue to bond the flurochemical part to the fiber. The important feature of the polymeric back bone is that it is capable of forming a durable film on the surface of the fiber. The principle of fluorocarbon polymer finishing is similar to that of non stick frying pans. Fluorocarbon polymers act as a plastic sheet on top of the fabric and any liquid coming in contact is repelled and cannot pass through the barrier. The liquid beads up and roll off the fabric and can be easily wicked or blotted off with a absorbent towel.

3.2.3. Mechanism of repellency

Repellent finishes achieve their properties by reducing the free energy at fiber surfaces. If the adhesive interactions between a fiber and a drop of liquid placed on the fiber are greater than the internal cohesive interaction within the liquid, the drop will spread. If the adhesive interactions between the fiber and the liquid are less than the internal cohesive interactions within the liquid, the drop will not spread. Surfaces that exhibit low interactions with liquids are referred to as low energy surfaces.

If the critical surface tension of solid is greater than or equal to the surface tension of liquid, the liquid will wet the fabric. If the critical surface tension of the solid is less than the surface tension of the liquid, the fabric will repel the liquid. Thus water repellency can be obtained in case the critical surface tension of solid is smaller than the surface tension of liquid. When cotton is treated with FCP, water repellent in advance between them changes too. Critical surface tension of water repellent finished cotton is less than the surface tension of water. Low energy surfaces also provide a measure of dry soil repellency by preventing soil particles from strongly adhering to fiber surfaces. This low interaction allows the soil particles to be easily dislodged and removed by mechanical action.

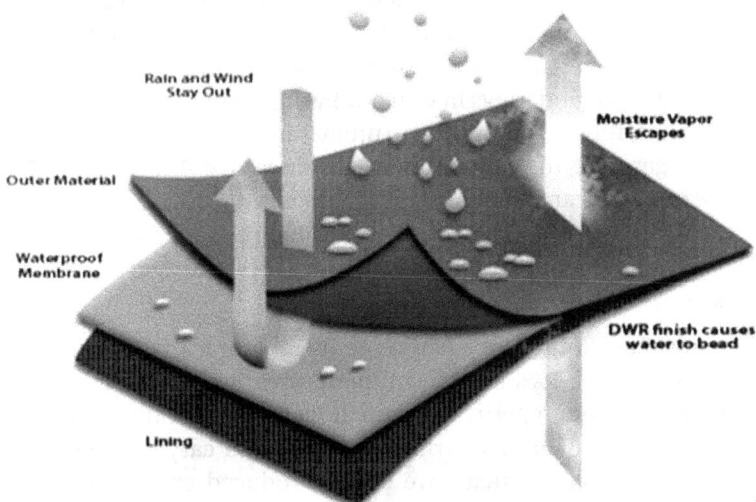

Fig. 3.1: Mechanism of repellency

Water proofing of the fabrics may be divided into two large classes:

1.   Processes in which interstices of the cloth as well as the, surface of the fibers, are covered with a film or skin so that the goods & not-only water shedding but impermeable to air and moisture.

2.   Processes whereby the fibres are made water repellent through coating with hydrophobic substance or by a chemical reaction, but the fabric remains porous to air, *i.e.* ventile.

The energy of the surface depends on the presence of fluorocarbon groups on it.Other finishing auxiliaries used with flurochemical polymers are

3.2.4. Cross linker

These compounds can be resins like DMDHEU or others to provide durability of the finish.

3.2.5. Extenders

An extender is less expensive aliphatic or wax waterrepellent that can be used to boost the performance and reduce the amount of flurochemical.

3.2.6. Non Rewetting agent

A fugitive wetting agent such as Isopropyl alcohol is added along with flurochemical polymer to assist wetting of the substrate. These fugitive wetting agents evaporate or flash off during curing. Conventional wetting agents should not be used, as they will remain on the fabric after curing and interfere with water and oil repellency.

3.2.7. New Generation Flurochemicals

Conventional fluorinated polymers including esters or amides of polyacrylic acids are either stable emulsions or dispersions for addition to aqueous pad baths. While, these products impart good resistance to soiling and staining, these are easily removed after several launderings in water or by dry cleaning. Garments treated with these flurochemical finishes are subject to premature disposal, since once the finish is depleted on the garment, the garment is usually discarded. New generation products to produce water, stain and soilrepellent repellency are based on flurosurfactants, which are capable of with standing numerous washing in water or dry cleanings. These new molecules are based on Perfluroalkyl hydroxyalkyl siloxane or the flurosilicone compounds.

The advantage of recent advancements in fluorocarbon chemistries is that the finish, when applied does not affect other properties of the fabric. For example, the technology adds stain repel/release functionality but permits cotton and cotton blended fabrics to maintain their wrinkle resistant and easy care properties. Some stain protection technologies that have been introduced provide dual action stain protection, as they impart soil repellency combined with stain release technologies.

These advancements in stain protection have been introduced as the new generation water and oilrepellent finishes. A dual action stainrepellent/stainrepellent technology function by repelling water based stains, at the same time, allowing soils that become stains when they penetrate the finish to be released.

Fluorocarbon polymers are used where very high performance and value added finishes are desired on 100% cotton fabrics. Other end uses of these polymers are acid and alkali protection, Alcohol and Petrol repellency, besides water and oil repellency. For end uses such as outer wear and rain wear, passing the rain test is required, which severely limits the fabrics that can be used to those with tighter construction. For technical outer wear tests more severe, than the rain test may be required such as Bundessmann and Hydrostatic pressure test.

3.3. Flame Retardants

As the whole environment is going highly technical and risky, the demand for specially treated textile such as flame resistant fabric has grown significantly. In the process of meeting with these demands, synthetic fiber has played a significant role. However, along with many advantages, these synthetic fabrics are also prone to fire. Whether it is concerned with the various electrical or electronics items in offices or dealing with highly flammable materials in other places including hotels, hospitals and even homes, the need for protective clothing is felt everywhere. The textile industry has found the solution by developing flame retardant finish for synthetic fibers like polyester fabrics, nylon fabrics, polypropylene fabrics *etc*. By applying flame retardants, fabrics are made flame resistant.

3.3.1. Definition of Flame Retardant

Flame retardants are materials that have the quality of inhibiting or resisting the spread of fire. Textile is highly ignitable and contributes to rapid fire spread. However, the ignitable property of a textile can be considerably reduced by any one of the three methods- by using inorganic materials such as Asbestos, Glass etc; by chemically treating the textile with Flame Retardant chemicals; and by modifying the polymer.

3.3.2. Categories of Flame Retardants

There are many categories in which flame retardants can be divided. The major categories among them include:

❖ Tetrakis (hydroxymethyl) phosphonium salts that are made by passing phosphine gas through a solution of formaldehyde and a mineral acid like hydrochloric acid. This category is mostly used as flame retardants for textiles.

❖ Minerals like asbestos, compounds such as aluminum hydroxide, magnesium hydroxide, antimony trioxide different hydrates, red phosphorus, and boron compounds, mostly borates. *etc*.

❖ Synthetic materials, usually halocarbons which include organochlorines such as polychlorinated biphenyls (PCBs), chlorendic acid derivates and chlorinated paraffins; organobromines such as polybrominated diphenyl ether (PBDEs), organophosphates in the form of halogenated phosphorus compounds and others.

3.3.3. Types of flame retardants

❖ Brominated flame retardants
❖ Chlorinated flame retardants
❖ Phosphorous-containing flame retardants (Phosphate ester such as Tri phenyl phosphate)
❖ Nitrogen-containing flame retardants (i.e. Melamines)
❖ Inorganic flame retardants.

Other method of classifying Flame Retardants is to divide them as Inorganic, Organo Phosphorous, Halogenated organic and Nitrogen based compounds. Halogenated organic flame retardants are further classified as having either Chlorine or Bromine which is popularly known as Brominated Flame Retardants (BFR)

3.3.4. Working of Flame Retardants

Flame retardant chemicals that are applied to fabrics are intended to inhibit or suppress the combustion process. These fire retardants interfere with combustion at different stages of the process like during heating, decomposition, ignition or spreading of flame. For understanding how flame retardants resist fire, first it should be known how a textile is heated up, catches fire and contributes in spreading it. As with any matter, a textile fabric exposed to a heat source experiences rise in temperature. If the temperature of the fire source is high enough and the net rate of heat transfer to the fabric is great, pyrolytic decomposition of the fiber substrate occurs. The products of this decomposition include combustible gases, non combustible gases and carbonaceous char. The combustible gases mix with the surrounding air and its oxygen. The mixture ignites, yielding a flame. It happens when the composition of textile and the temperature, both are favorable. Part of the heat generated within the flame is transferred to the fabric to sustain the burning process and part is lost to the surroundings. Now, if the textile is flame resistant then the flame retardant can act physically and/or chemically by interfering at particular stages of burning. There are different mechanisms of flame retardants.

3.3.5. Mechanisms of Flame Retardants

Flame retardants can act physically or chemically and sometimes both by physically and chemically interfering at particular stages of burning. The different mechanisms are:

3.3.5.1 Endothermic Degradation

Certain compounds break down endothermically when they are subjected to high temperatures. Magnesium and aluminium hydroxides are such examples.

Various hydrates also act similarly. The reaction takes off heat from the surroundings, thus cooling the material.

3.3.5.2 Dilution of Fuel

Substances, which evolve inert gases on decomposition, dilute the fuel in the solid and gaseous phases. Inert fillers, *eg.* talc or calcium carbonate, act as diluents, lowering the combustible portion of the material, thus lowering the amount of heat per volume of material that it can produce while burning. Thus the concentrations of combustible gases fall under the ignition limit.

3.3.5.3 Thermal Shielding

A thermal insulation barrier is created between the burning and the yet-to-burn parts. In tumescent additives are sometimes applied that turn the polymer into a carbonized foam, resultantly separating the flame from the material and slowing down the heat transfer to the unburned fuel.

3.3.5.4 Dilution of Gas Phase

Inert gases, mostly carbon dioxide and water, act as diluent of the combustible gases, lowering their partial pressures and the partial pressure of oxygen, thus slowing the reaction rate. These gases are produced by thermal degradation of some materials.

3.3.5.5 Gas Phase Radical Quenching

Chlorinated and brominated materials undergo thermal degradation and release hydrogen chloride and hydrogen bromide. These react with the highly reactive H. and OH. radicals in the flame, resulting in an inactive molecule and a Cl. or Br. radical. The halogen radical has much lower energy than H. or OH. and thus has much lower potential to propagate the radical oxidation reactions of combustion. Antimony compounds tend to act in synergy with halogenated flame retardants. The HCl and HBr released during burning are highly corrosive, which has reliability implications for objects subjected to the released smoke.

3.3.5.6 Chemical Effect Gas Phase

The flame retardant or their degradation products stop the radical mechanism of the combustion process that takes place in the gas phase. The exothermic processes, which occur in the flame, are thus stopped, the system cools down, the supply of flammable gases is reduced and eventually completely suppressed. The high-reactive radicals HO· and H· can react in the gas phase with other radicals, such as halogenated radicals X· resulted from flame retardant degradation. Less reactive radicals which decrease the kinetics of the combustion are created.

$$R\text{-}X + P\text{-}H \rightarrow H\text{-}X + R\text{-}P$$

$$H\text{-}X + H. \rightarrow H_2 + X.$$

$$H\text{-}Z + OH. \rightarrow H_2O + X.$$

Flame inhibition studies have shown that the effectiveness decreases as follow: **HI>HBr>HCl>HF.**

$$Sb_2O_3 + 6\,HX \rightleftharpoons 2\,SbX_3 + 3\,H_2O$$

$$SbX_3 + H^\cdot \rightleftharpoons SbX_2 + HX$$

$$SbX_2 + H^\cdot \rightleftharpoons SbX + HX$$

$$SbX + H^\cdot \rightleftharpoons Sb + HX$$

$$Sb + O^\cdot \rightleftharpoons SbO^\cdot$$

$$SbO^\cdot + H^\cdot \rightleftharpoons SbOH$$

$$SbOH + H^\cdot \rightleftharpoons SbO^\cdot + H_2$$

3.3.5.7 Mechanism of action of halogenated flame retardants

Brominated compounds and chlorinated organic compounds are generally used because iodides are thermally unstable at processing temperature and effectiveness of fluorides is too low. The choice depends on polymer type. The behaviour of the halogenated fire retardant in processing conditions (stability, melting, distribution, etc...) and/or effect on properties and long-term stability of the resulting material are among the criteria that have to be considered. Moreover it is particularly recommended to use an additive that produces halide to the flame at the same range of temperature of polymer degradation into combustible volatile products. Then, fuel and inhibitor would both reach the gas phase according to the right place at the right time principle. The most effective fire retardant (FR) polymeric materials are halogen-based polymer (PVC, CPVC, FEP, PVDF...) and additives (CP, TBBA, DECA, BEOs...).

However the improvement of fire- performance depends on the type of fire tests i.e. the application. They perfectly illustrate the previously described chemical modes of action. Severe perturbations of the kinetic mechanism of the combustion lead to incomplete combustion.

3.3.5.8 Synergism with Antimony trioxide (Sb_2O_3)

To be efficient the trapping free radicals needs to reach the flame in gaz phase. Addition of antimony trioxide allows formation of volatile antimony species (antimony halides or antimonyoxyhalide) capable to interrupt the combustion process by inhibiting H* radicals via a serie of reactions proposed bellow. This phenomenon explains the synergistic effect between halogenated compounds and Sb_2O_3. For most applications, these two ingredients are present in the formulations.

3.3.5.9 Physical Effects

3.3.5.9.1 Formation of a protective layer

The additives can form a shield with low thermal conductivity, through an external heat flux, that can reduce the heat transfer Delta H2 (from the heat source to the material). It then reduces the degradation rate of the polymer and decreases the fuel flow (pyrolysis gases from the degradation of the material) that feeds the flame. Phosphorous additives may act the same way. Their pyrolysis leads to thermally stable pyro- or polyphosphoric compounds which form a protective vitreous barrier. The same mechanism can be observed using boric acid based additives, **zinc borates** or low melting glasses.

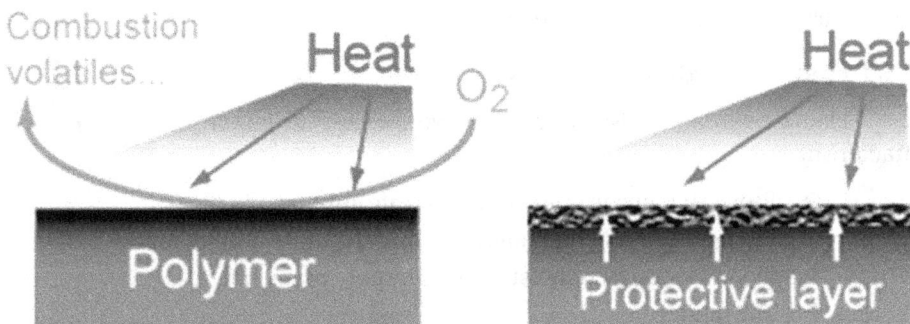

Fig. 3.2: Formation of protective layer inhibiting, combustion and volatiles

3.3.5.9.2 Cooling effect

The degradation reactions of the additive can influence the energy balance of combustion. The additive can degrade endothermally which cools the substrate to a temperature which is below the one required for sustaining the combustion process. Different metal hydroxides follow this principle and its efficiency depends on the amount incorporated in the polymer.

3.3.5.9.3 Dilution

The incorporation of inert substances (e.g. fillers such as talc or chalk) and additives (which evolve as inert gases on decomposition) dilutes the fuel in the solid and gaseous phases so that the lower ignition limit of the gas mixture is not reached. In recent work, the isolating effect of a high amount of ash (resulting from certain silica-based fillers) has been shown in fire-retarded systems. Moreover, it highlights also an opposite effect as thermal degradation of the polymer in the bulk is increased by heat conductivity of the filled material.

3.3.6. Application of Flame Retardants on Textiles

Flame Retardants on fabric can be applied through conventional padding, padding with multiple dips and nips. If followed by 30 to 60 seconds dwell, it gives good results. The pH of the pad bath is optimally kept at approximately 5.0. The amount of flame retardant required depends primarily on the fabric type, application conditions, and test criteria required to be met with. Screening experiments should be conducted to determine the minimum application level for a fabric. One of the most common processes for applying Flame Retardants on cotton fabrics is the Precondensate/NH_3 process. One of several phosphoniums precondensates is applied after which the fabric is cured with ammonia. Then it is oxidized with hydrogen peroxide. Precondensate is the Tetrakis-hydroxymethyl phosphonium salt pre-reacted with urea or another nitrogenous material. The amount of anhydrous sodium acetate is approximately 4% of the amount of precondensate used. Some precondensates are formulated along with the sodium acetate. Softeners are also added along with precondensates. A critical factor in the successful application of precondensate/NH3 flame retardant is the control of fabric moisture before ammoniation. Generally, moisture levels between 10% and 20% give good results.

3.3.6.1 Flame Retardants Finishes

Flame-retardant finishes provide textiles with an important performance characteristic.

❖ Protection of consumers from unsafe apparel
❖ Firefighters and emergency personnel require protection
❖ Floor coverings, upholstery and drapery protection
❖ The military
❖ The airline industry

3.3.7. Flame Retardants for Cellulose

3.3.7.1 Non durable:

1. Inorganic salts have long been known to provide flame retardancy on cellulosic material that will not be exposed to water, rain or perspiration.
2. The French chemist Gay-Lussac proposed a borax and ammonium sulfate treatment as a flame retardant for cotton in 1820.
3. Today, a mixture of boric acid and borax is still an effective flame retardant for cotton at ~ 10 % solids add-on.
4. Ammonium salts of strong acids, especially phosphoric acid (P/N synergism) are particularly useful as nondurable flame retardants for cellulose. Example:

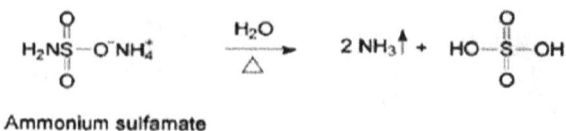

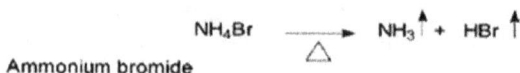

$$(NH_4)_2HPO_4 \xrightarrow{\triangle} 2NH_3\uparrow + HO-\underset{\underset{OH}{|}}{\overset{\overset{O}{\|}}{P}}-OH$$

Diammonium phosphate

$$H_2N\underset{\underset{O}{\|}}{\overset{\overset{O}{\|}}{S}}-O^-NH_4^+ \xrightarrow[\triangle]{H_2O} 2NH_3\uparrow + HO-\underset{\underset{O}{\|}}{\overset{\overset{O}{\|}}{S}}-OH$$

Ammonium sulfamate

$$NH_4Br \xrightarrow{\triangle} NH_3\uparrow + HBr\uparrow$$

Ammonium bromide

Thermal decomposition of ammonium salts.

3.3.7.2 Durable:

1. The most successful durable flame retardants for cellulose are based on
    - ❖ Phosphorous- and nitrogen-containing chemical systems .
    - ❖ That can react with the fibre or form crosslinked structures on the fibre.
2. The key ingredient of one of these finishes is
    - ❖ Tetrakis(hydroxymethyl)phosphonium chloride (THPC),
    - ❖ Made from phosphine, formaldehyde and hydrochloric acid

$$PH_3 + \underset{\underset{H \ \ H}{\overset{\|}{C}}}{\overset{O}{}} + HCl \rightleftharpoons \overset{Cl^-}{P^+(CH_2OH)_4}$$

Phosphine   Formaldehyde   Tetrakis (hydroxymethyl) phosphonium Chloride (THPC)

Synthesis of THPC

3.3.7.3 Mechanism of combustion of fire:

Combustion is an exothermic process that requires three components

1. Heat
2. Oxygen
3. A suitable fuel
    - ❖ When left unchecked, combustion becomes self catalyzing and will continue until the oxygen, the fuel supply or the excess heat is depleted.

Combustion cycle for fibres

- ❖ When heat is applied, the fiber's temperature increases until the pyrolysis temperature, Tp, is reached. At this temperature, the fiber undergoes irreversible chemical changes, producing non flammable gases (carbon dioxide, water vapor and the higher oxides of nitrogen and sulfur), carbonaceous char, tars (liquid condensates) and flammable gases (carbon monoxide, hydrogen and many oxidisable organic molecules).

❖ As the temperature continues to rise, the tars also pyrolyse, producing, more non- flammable gases, char and flammable gases. Eventually, the combustion temperature, Tc, is achieved. At this point, the flammable gases combine with oxygen in process called combustion, which is a series of gas phase free radical reactions.

$$H^\bullet + O_2 \rightleftharpoons HO^\bullet + O^\bullet$$

$$O^\bullet + H_2 \rightleftharpoons HO^\bullet + H^\bullet$$

$$HO^\bullet + CO \rightleftharpoons CO_2 + H^\bullet$$

Some free radical combustion reactions

❖ These reactions are highly exothermic and produce large amounts of heat and light. The heat generated by the combustion process provides the additional thermal energy needed to continue the pyrolysis of the fiber, thereby supplying one more flammable gases for combustion and perpetuating the reaction. The burning behavior of textiles is determined more by the speed or rate of heat release than by the amount of this heat.

3.3.8. Various approaches used for disruption of combustion cycle

The various methods for disruption of combustion cycle are:

❖ To provide a heat sink on or in the fiber by use of materials that thermally decomposes through strongly endothermic reactions. If enough heat can be absorbed by these reactions, the pyrolysis temperature of the fiber is not reached and no combustion takes place. Examples of this method are the use of aluminium hydroxide or 'alumina trihydrate' and calcium carbonate as fillers in polymers and coatings.

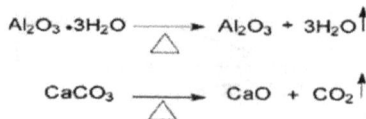

$$Al_2O_3 \cdot 3H_2O \xrightarrow{\triangle} Al_2O_3 + 3H_2O\uparrow$$

$$CaCO_3 \xrightarrow{\triangle} CaO + CO_2\uparrow$$

Endothermic decompostion reactions

❖ To apply a material that forms an insulating layer around the fiber at temperatures below the fiber pyrolysis temperature. Boric acid and its hydrated salts function in this capacity. Fig 8.4

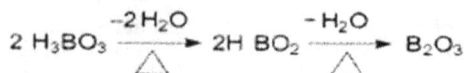

$$2\ H_3BO_3 \xrightarrow[\triangle]{-2\,H_2O} 2H\ BO_2 \xrightarrow[\triangle]{-\,H_2O} B_2O_3$$

Formation of formed glass

❖ When heated, these low melting compounds release water vapor and produce foamed glassy surface on the fiber, insulating the fiber from the applied heat and oxygen. C. To achieve flame retardancy is to influence the pyrolysis reaction to produce less flammable volatiles and more residual char. This 'condensed phase' mechanism can be seen in the action of phosphorous- containing flame retardants which, after having produced phosphoric acid through thermal decomposition, crosslink with hydroxyl-containing polymers thereby altering the pyrolysis to yield less flammable by-products.

Crosslinking with phosphoric acid

But there is also other explanation for the first step of this dehydration, including single esterification without cross linking, for example, of the primary hydroxyl group in the C-6position of the cellulose units. The phosphorous esters catalyze the dehydration,

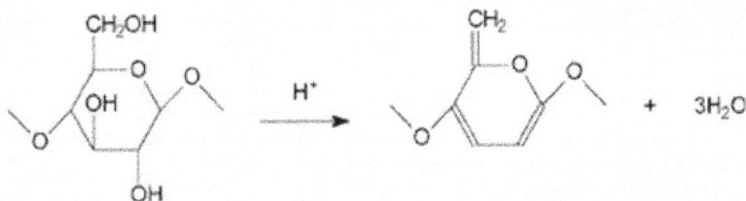

Dehydration of cellulose by strong acids

And prevent the formation of undesired laevoglucose, the precursor of flammable volatiles.

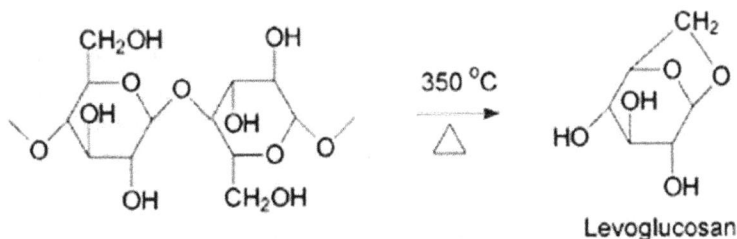

Levoglucosan

Thermal degradation of cellulose

3.3.9. Comparison of Condensed and Gas Phase Mechanism

Type of mechanism	Condensed phase	Gas phase
Type of chemistry involved	Pyrolysis chemistry	Flame chemistry
Typical type of synergism	P/N	Sb/Br or Sb/Cl
Effective for fiber type	Mainly cellulose, also wool, catalyzing their dehydration to char	All kinds of fibers, because their flame chemistry is similar (radical transfer reactions)
Particularities	Very effective because dehydration and carbonization decrease the formation of burnable volatiles	Fixation with binder changes textiles properties such as handle and drape, preferably for back coating for example of furnishing fabrics and carpets
Application process	If for durable flame retardancy then demanding multi step process	Relatively simple, standard methods of coating, but viscosity control is important
Environment toxicity	With durable flame retardancy, formaldehyde emission during curing and after finishing,phosphorous compounds in the waste water	Antimony oxide and organic halogen donators (DBDPO and HCBC) are discussed as problems (for eg.Possibility of generating poly halogenated dioxins and furans)

3.4. Anti microbial finishes

Textiles have always played a central role in the evolution of human culture by being at the forefront of both technological and artistic development. The protective aspects of textile have provided the most textile ground for innovative developments. Hygiene has acquired importance in recent years. Odour has become an important factor. Unpleasant odour can arise from the acquisition of a variety of compounds produced in bodily fluids such as perspiration. Consumers are looking for solutions to odour and microbial problem and the unique benefits provided by antimicrobial finish. Microorganism growth is another factor that has resulted in development of antimicrobial finish. Microbial infestation poses danger to both living and non-living matters. Microorganisms cause problems with textile raw materials and processing chemicals, wet processes in the mills, roll or bulk goods in storage, finished goods in storage and transport, and goods as the consumer uses them. Obnoxious smell form the inner garments such as socks, spread of diseases, staining and degradation of textiles are some of the detrimental effects of bad microbes. The consumers are now increasingly aware of the hygienic life style and there is a necessity and expectation for a wide range of textile products finished with antimicrobial properties.

Moth, mildew, fungus, yeast, and bacteria (microorganisms) are part of our everyday lives. There are both good and bad types of microorganisms. The thousands of species of microorganisms that exist are found everywhere in the environment and on our bodies. These organisms impact producers, retailers, and users of all kinds of products. The scope of this reaches from whole buildings, building materials, people, equipment, processes, production of textiles, storage and transport of textiles, and users of textiles. Understanding microorganisms, which they are, where they come from, and why they grow on certain materials provides us a basis for controlling them and their negative effects. This control capability, with the right technology, can provide for a valuable feature on a wide range of textiles. The inherent properties of the textile fibres provide room for the growth of microorganisms. Besides, the structure of the substrates and the chemical processes may induce the growth of microbes. Humid and warm environment still aggravate the problem. Infestation by microbes cause cross infection by pathogens and development odour where the fabric is worn next to skin. In addition, the staining and loss of the performance properties of textile substrates are the results of microbial attack. Basically, with a view to protect the wearer and the textile substrate itself antimicrobial finish is applied to textile materials. Antimicrobial textile products continue to increase in popularity as demand for fresh smelling, skin friendly, high performance fabrics goes on. Modern performance fabrics are required in many specialist applications, sports textile is one example. These need to exhibit high degrees of performance in terms of longevity and durability, and by imparting antimicrobial properties to the fabric. These properties can be improved as well as increasing the comfort and hygiene factor making them more pleasant to wear. Odour can be neutralized and skin problems caused by microbial growth reduced thus emphasizing the hygiene nature of the treated product.

3.4.1. Microbes or micro-organisms

Microbes are the tiniest creatures not seen by the naked eye. They include a variety of micro-organisms like Bacteria, Fungi, Algae and viruses. Bacteria are uni-cellular organisms, which grow very rapidly under warmth and moisture. Further, sub divisions in the bacteria family are Gram positive (Staphylococcus aureus), Gram negative (E-Coli), spore bearing or non-spore bearing type. Some specific types of bacteria are pathogenic and cause cross infection. Fungi, molds or mildew are complex organisms with slow growth rate. They stain the fabric and deteriorate the performance properties of the fabrics. Fungi are active at a pH level of 6.5. Algae are typical microorganisms, which are either fungal or bacterial. Algae require continuous sources of water and sunlight to grow and develop darker stains on the fabrics. Algae are active in the PH range of 7.0-8.0. Dust mites are eight legged creatures and occupy the household textiles such as blankets bed linen, pillows, mattresses and carpets. The dust mites feed on human skin cells and liberated waste products can cause allergic reactions and respiratory disorders.

3.4.2. Sources of microbes

- ❖ In the air we breath
- ❖ In the soil
- ❖ In our skin and bodies
- ❖ Everywhere

3.4.3. Ideal Conditions For microbial Growth

- ❖ Food
- ❖ Warm temperature
- ❖ Moisture (Humidity, Spills)
- ❖ Receptive surface (skin, fabric)

3.4.4. Antimicrobials

Antimicrobials control, destroy or suppress the growth of microorganisms and their negative effects of odour, staining and deterioration.

3.4.5. Antimicrobial finishes

Antimicrobials do not all work the same. The vast majority of antimicrobials work by leaching or moving from the surface on which they are applied. This is the mechanism used by leaching antimicrobials to poison a microorganism. Such chemicals have been used for decades in agricultural applications with mixed results. Besides affecting durability and useful life, leaching technologies have the potential to cause a variety of other problems when used in garments. These include their negative effects because, they can contact the skin and potentially effect the normal skin bacteria, cross the skin barrier, and/or have the potential to cause rashes and other skin irritations. A more serious problem with leaching technologies has to do with their allowing for the adaptation of microorganisms. An antimicrobial with a completely different mode of action than the leaching technologies is a molecularly bonded unconventional technology. The bound unconventional antimicrobial technology, an organofunctional silane, has a mode of action that relies on the technology remaining affixed to the substrate killing microorganisms as they contact the surface to which it is applied. Effective levels of this technology do not leach or diminish over time. When applied, the technology actually polymerizes with the substrate making the surface antimicrobial. This type of antimicrobial technology is used in textiles that are likely to have human contact or where durability is of value.

3.4.6. Necessity of Antimicrobial Finishes

Antimicrobial treatment for textile materials is necessary to fulfill the following objectives:

- ❖ To control microorganisms
- ❖ To reduce odour from perspiration, stains and other soil on textile material
- ❖ To reduce the risk of cross infection being carried by feet from ward to ward in hospital
- ❖ To control spread of disease and danger of infection following injury

❖ To control the deterioration of textiles particularly fabrics made from natural fibre caused by mildew

3.4.7. Requirements for Antimicrobial Finish

Textile materials in particular, the garments are more susceptible to wear and tear. It is important to take into account the impact of stress strain, thermal and mechanical effects on the finished substrates. The following requirements need to be satisfied to obtain maximum benefits out of the finish:

❖ Durability to washing, dry cleaning and hot pressing
❖ Selective activity to undesirable microorganisms
❖ Should not produce harmful effects to the manufacturer, user and the environment
❖ Should comply with the statutory requirements of regulating agencies
❖ Compatibility with the chemical processes
❖ Easy method of application
❖ No deterioration of fabric quality
❖ Resistant to body fluids
❖ Resistant to disinfections/sterilization.

3.4.8. Antimicrobial Finishing Methodologies

The antimicrobial agents can be applied to the textile substrates by exhaust, pad-dry-cure, coating, spray and foam techniques. The substances can also be applied by directly adding into the fibre spinning dope. It is claimed that the commercial agents can be applied online during the dyeing and finishing operations. Various methods for improving the durability of the finish include:

❖ Insolubilisation of the active substances in/on the fibre
❖ Treating the fibre with resin, condensates or cross linking agents
❖ Micro encapsulation of the antimicrobial agents with the fibre matrix
❖ Coating the fibre surface
❖ Chemical modification of the fibre by covalent bond formation
❖ Use of graft polymers, homo polymers and/or co polymerization on to the fibre.

3.4.9. Mechanism of antimicrobial activity

Negative effect on the vitality of the microorganisms is generally referred to as antimicrobial. The degree of activity is differentiated by the term cidal that indicates significant destruction of microbes and the term ecstatic represents inhibition of microbial growth without much destruction. The differentiation of antimicrobial activity is given in the diagram.

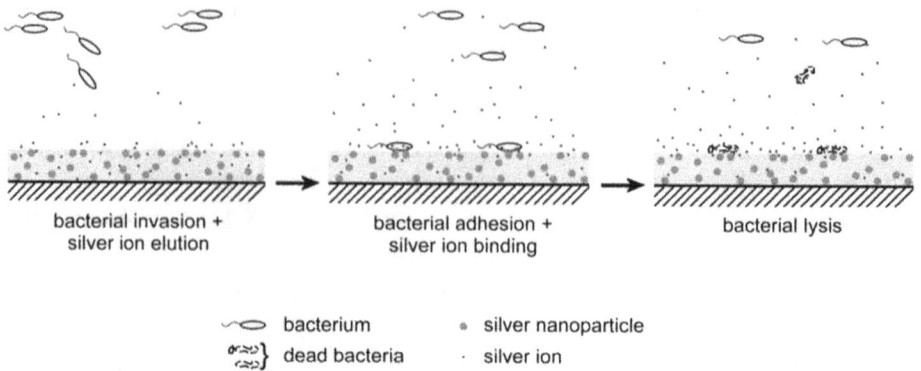

bacterial invasion + silver ion elution	bacterial adhesion + silver ion binding	bacterial lysis

∼○ bacterium   • silver nanoparticle

dead bacteria   · silver ion

The activity, which affects the bacteria, is known as antibacterial and that of fungi is antimycotic. The antimicrobial substances function in different ways. In the conventional leaching type of finish, the species diffuse and poison the microbes to kill. This type of finish shows poor durability and may cause health problems. The non-leaching type or bio-static finish shows good durability and may not provoke any health problems. A large number of textiles with antimicrobial finish function by diffusion type. The rate of diffusion has a direct effect on the effectiveness of the finish. For example, in the ion exchange process, the release of the active substances is at a slower rate compared to direct diffusion ad hence, has a weaker effect. Similarly, in the case of antimicrobial modifications where the active substances are not released from the fibre surface and so less effective. They are active only when they come in contact with microorganisms.

Considering the medical, toxicological and ecological principles has developed these so called new technologies. The antimicrobial textiles can be classified into two categories, namely, passive and active based on their activity against microorganisms. Passive materials do not contain any active substances but their surface structure (Lotus effect) produces negative effect on the living conditions of microorganisms (Anti-adhesive effect). Materials containing active antimicrobial substances act upon either in or on the cell.

3.4.10. Antimicrobial Function & Adaptation

Antimicrobials primarily function in two different ways. The conventional leaching types of antimicrobials leave the textile and chemically enter or react with the microorganism acting as a poison. The unconventional bound antimicrobial stays affixed to the textile and, on a molecular scale, physically stabs (the membrane) and electrocutes (the biochemical in the membrane) the microorganism on contact to kill it. Like an arrow shot from a bow or bullet shot from a gun, leaching antimicrobials are often effective, but they are used up in the process of working or wasted in random misses. Some companies incorporate leaching technologies into fibers and slow the release rate to extend the useful life of the antimicrobial or even add them to chemical binders and claim they are now bound.

Whether leaching antimicrobials are extruded into the fiber, placed in a binder or simply added as a finish to fabrics or finished goods, they all function the same. In all cases leaching antimicrobial technologies provide a killing field or zone of inhibition. This zone exists in real-world uses if it is assumed that the right conditions exist for leaching of a lethal dose at the time that it is needed. The zone of inhibition is the area around the treated substrate into which the antimicrobial chemistry leaches or moves to, killing or inhibiting microorganisms. This killing or inhibiting action of a leaching antimicrobial is witnessed when an AATCC 147 test or other zone on inhibition test is run. These tests measure the zone of inhibition created by a leaching antimicrobial and clearly defines the area where the antimicrobial has come off the substrate and killed the microorganisms in the agar. Such a phenomenon can be seen in Figure1. This Figure shows the difference between the leaching and the non-leaching antimicrobial treatments on textiles both as first treated and then after five household launderings.

3.4.11. Benefits of Antimicrobial Textiles

A wide range textile product is now available for the benefit of the consumer. Initially, the primary objective of the finish was to protect textiles from being affected by microbes particularly fungi. Uniforms, tents, defense textiles and technical textiles, such as, geo-textiles have therefore all been finished using antimicrobial agents. Later, the home textiles, such as, curtains coverings, and bath mats came with antimicrobial finish. The application of the finish is now extended to textiles used for outdoor, healthcare sector, sports and leisure. Novel technologies in antimicrobial finishing are successfully employed in non-woven sector especially in medical textiles. Textile fibres with built-in antimicrobial properties will also serve the purpose alone or in blends with other fibres. Bioactive fibre is a modified form of the finish, which includes chemotherapeutics in their structure, i.e., synthetic drugs of bactericidal and fungicidal qualities. These fibres are not only used in medicine and health prophylaxis applications but also for manufacturing textile products of daily use and technical textiles. The field of application of the bioactive fibres includes sanitary materials, dressing materials, surgical threads, materials for filtration of gases and liquids, air conditioning and ventilation, constructional materials, special materials for food industry, pharmaceutical industry, footwear industry, clothing industry, automotive industry *etc.*

❖ To benefit from the consumer demand for antimicrobial/antibacterial products and for the antibacterial and antifungal performance needs of the textile world, manufacturers have a choice. In choosing, they should utilize a treatment that provides for an odor reduction/ antibacterial claim and an antimicrobial finish for their textile products consistent with their claims and the needs of their target consumers. This selection should be done by considering:

❖ Adopting an antimicrobial technology with a proven history of use. This will help shorten the timelines in bringing products with an antibacterial/antifungal/odor-reducing, antimicrobial feature to market.

❖ Adopting a non-leaching antimicrobial that doesn't pose the risk of crossing the skin barrier. If it creates a zone of inhibition it leaches or moves and has the potential to cause problems.

❖ Adopting a non-leaching antimicrobial that does not pose the risk of creating adaptative resistant microorganisms.

❖ Adopting an antimicrobial technology that can have its proper application tested for at the mill or at the retailers. A verifiable quality assurance program should be a key component of any application process.

❖ Adopting an antimicrobial technology that has technical and marketing support.

❖ Numerous retail buyers have stated that the antimicrobial/antibacterial feature is quickly moving to a standard requirement for the products that they buy. Manufacturers that don't currently treat fabrics with a durable antimicrobial finish should consider shielding their products from eroding value by incorporating microbial control. As manufacturers look to enhance the value of their products they should recognize antimicrobial finishes as a feature with a future and the future is now.

An anti-bacterial surface contains an antibacterial agent that opposes the ability of micro-organisms to grow on textile materials.

A. Anti-bacterial Agent

Product is design to resists the growth or to kill the bacteria.

B. Anti-Bacterial Finish

Treatment designs to prevent the growth of bacteria to reduce the number of bacteria or to kill bacteria.

C. Anti-Bacterial activity

Activity of an anti-bacterial finishes used to resists the growth or to reduce the number of bacteria.

Chemical Formula:

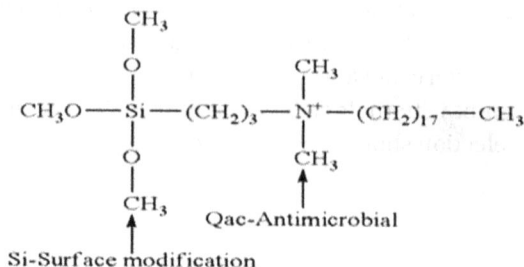

$$CH_3O - Si - (CH_2)_3 - N^+ - (CH_2)_{17} - CH_3$$

Qac-Antimicrobial

Si-Surface modification

3.4.12. Finishing Agents

3.4.12.1 Quaternary Ammonium

Quaternary Ammonium directly target to the microbial surface and the bacterial layers. For attaining a good response or excellent efficiency quaternary ammonium is used in a polymeric as monomeric link.

Quaternary Ammonium contains both:

- ❖ Perfluoroalkyl Group
- ❖ Diallyl Group

These both salts are suitable finishing agents and resists the micro-organisms and bacteria from the surface of the fabric. Further more it also prevents soil, oil, blood and water to penetrate in the fabric. These salts cannot only increase the anti-bacterial properties also enhance the properties of applications.

3.4.12.2 Triclosan

Triclosan is an antiseptic and disinfectant agent. Triclosan is a derivate of phenol. It also used in toothpaste and cosmetics. It has a good resistance against positive gram bacteria, negative gram bacteria and mites. In this agent benzyl Benzoate compound has an important role, which is used in spray or powder. It has a great effect on mites, molds and bacteria. It is non-toxic compound, its anti-bacterial properties due to the presence of benzyl benzoate. It has a large number of consumers and widespread products like toothpaste, deodorants, soap, polymers, and fibers.

3.4.12.3 Metallic Salts

For cotton fabrics number of chemicals are used, these chemicals are toxic for bacteria, molds *etc.* They can form bond with fabric or move in freely state on the surface of the fabric. They also harm the bacteria by binding with intracellular proteins. As we know the phenomena of polyester extrusion method, before the nano-fiber formation. The natural fibers always treated with metals in finishing stage and a lot of techniques are now discovered for enhancing the uptake and durability of fabric. Cotton first treated with succinic acid, anhydride which reacts as ligand more metallic ions to improve the adsorption property of metallic salts and also provides protection to the fabric material against bacterial and microbial activity.

3.4.13. Mechanism of Anti-bacterial Finishes

Many chemical finishes area unit accustomed manufacture anti-bacterial and anti-microbial finishes. They are accustomed provide the properties to alternative textile materials. The product area unit divided into 2 major types:

- ❖ One kind consists of chemicals which will be thought-about as Controlled Discharged Mechanism. The anti-microbial is bit by bit discharged on the material surface or within the core of the material. The 'leaching' kind could be a style of anti-microbial and is incredibly effective against microbes on the fiber surface or in atmosphere. Once the reservoir is depleted than the end can now not work. And if the microbes are introduced on the atmosphere than which will interfere the atmosphere pollution or with alternative fascinating microbes like wastes.

❖ Second type of anti-bacterial finish consists of molecules that are chemically bond to fibers surfaces. These anti-microbial finishes can only control those microbes that are present or exists on the fabric surface, not in the surroundings. These are also called Bound Anti-Microbial because of their attachment to the fiber can potentially be grinded away, or became deactivated and loose long term durability.

These anti-microbial finishes can also control the growth and spread of microbes move properly called Biostats i.e. Bacteriostats or Fungistats. Products that actually kill the microbes are biocides i.e. bactericides, fungicides. Some are as follows:

1) Tributyltinoxide:

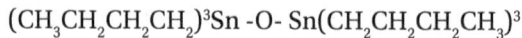

$$(CH_3CH_2CH_2CH_2)^3Sn -O- Sn(CH_2CH_2CH_2CH_3)^3$$

2) Dichlorophene:

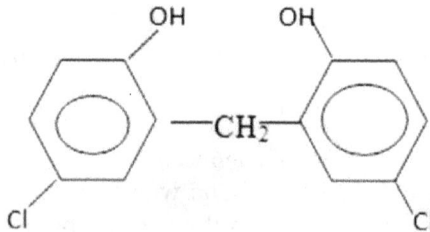

3) 3-Iodoprpynylbutyl Carbamate:

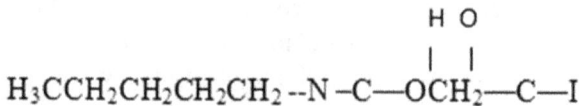

$$H_3CCH_2CH_2CH_2CH_2 --N -\overset{\displaystyle H}{\underset{\displaystyle |}{C}}-O\overset{\displaystyle O}{\underset{\displaystyle |}{C}}H_2—C—I$$

3.4.14. Essential Component of Anti Bacterial Finish:

1. Chitosan

Chitosan is a derivative of chitin, which is normally polysaccharide mainly resulting from the shells and shrimps. Chemically it can be designated as poly-β-(1$\rightarrow$4) D-Glucosamine. In addition to its antimicrobial activity, chitosan has some important advantages such as:

- ❖ Non toxicity
- ❖ Bio-Compatibility
- ❖ Bio-Degradable

To provide anti microbic impact for textiles chitosan are often used as finishing agent for surface modifications, principally of polyose, cellulose/polyester and wool fibers.

3.4.15. Working of Chitosan

Chitosan is a positively charged and soluble in acidic to neutral solutions because the amino groups in chitosan have a pKa of ~6.5. Its anti microbial function arises from its polycations nature, which is caused by protonation of the amino groups at the C-2 atom of the glucosamine units. Positive charged amino groups can bind to the negatively charged bacterial surface, resulting in disruption of the cell membrane and an increase in its permeability. Chitosan is also used to prevent protein synthesis.

3.4.16. Applications of Anti-Bacterial Finish

- ❖ Anti-bacterial finishes are employed in medical devices like medical tools, instruments, devices, machines.
- ❖ It is also used in health care sector, and devices.
- ❖ These finishes has important role in water purification system.
- ❖ In dental hospitals these finishes are profusely used for killing the germs and microorganism.
- ❖ These finishes are utilized in hospitals in an exceedingly textile section like : bed sheets, lab coats, gloves, and shoes.
- ❖ These finishes have a very important role in meditech.
- ❖ These finishes are also used in food packaging systems.

3.4.16.1 Manufacturing Companies

- ❖ Dmoz
- ❖ Bio Guard
- ❖ Par-Filters
- ❖ BarsanaHychem Industries
- ❖ JK- Texbond
- ❖ Gray 'C Implex
- ❖ Corner Stone

3.4.17 Trade Names

A. AEGIS (Eco Fresh)

These finishes area unit combine with water and so apply to any textile material; they will defend the fiber from bacterium, microbes and different fungi's. They are Eco friendly and simply bio-degradable.

B. AEGIS (Microbe Shields)

These finishes can resist the growth of dirt and odors due to molds, bacteria and mildew.

C. Agion

Agion finishes are anti-bacterial finishes, the technology provides built in protection by continuously resisting the growth of microbes.

D. AgUARDIAN

Finish is anti-bacterial and silver ion-exchange answer for poly ester materials.

E. Earth while

Earth while finish is an eco-smart fabrics natural organic and recycle.

As the population increases the hygienic problems and harmful diseases also come into being. It can affect the environment as well as the internal conditions of the human beings. To reduce these harmful and toxic diseases we have to take precautionary measures and protect the things from different parasites, bacteria, fungi and molds which we use in daily life. The Anti-Bacterial and Anti-microbial finish has overcome the fact of increasing the bacteria and parasites, by applying it at any of the thing which we used in our daily lives.

3.5. Antistatic Finish

Antistatic finishes are used for the removal in synthetic fibres of the unwanted effects of electrostatic charge produced during production and wear of fabrics and knits. Electrostatic charge causes an undesirable adhesive power and a resultant shabbiness. It is applied by means of an anti-static chemical treatment, the effect of which may be temporary or permanent. There are two types of Antistatic finish

1. Non-durable finishes
2. Durable finishes

3.5.1. Non-durable finishes

Non- durable antistatic agents are preferred for fiber and yarn processing finishes since ease of removal is important. Other important requirements of spin finish and fiber lubricants are heat resistance and oil solubility. This group of mostly hygroscopic materials includes surfactants, organic salts, glycols, polyethylene glycols, and polyelectrolyte, quaternary ammonium salts with fatty alkyl chains, polyethylene oxide compounds and esters of salts of alkyl phosphonium acids. The general requirements for non durable anti-static are:

❖ Low volatility
❖ Low flammability

❖ Non yellowing (heat stable)

❖ Non corrosive

❖ Low foaming

1. Esters of phosphoric acid form the largest group of non-durable antistats

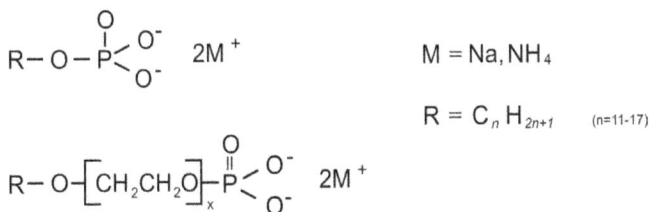

$$R-O-\overset{\overset{\textstyle O}{\|}}{P}\!\!<\!\!\overset{O^-}{\underset{O^-}{}}\quad 2M^+ \qquad\qquad M = Na, NH_4$$

$$R = C_n H_{2n+1} \quad {\scriptstyle (n=11\text{-}17)}$$

$$R-O-\!\!\left[CH_2CH_2O\right]_x\!\!-\overset{\overset{\textstyle O}{\|}}{P}\!\!<\!\!\overset{O^-}{\underset{O^-}{}}\quad 2M^+$$

Phosphoric ester antistats

The alkyl groups are usually derived from fatty acids. Ethoxylated fatty alcohols are also used to form the esters. The durability of these phosphoric acid esters increases with molecular size.

2. Quaternary ammonium compounds are the next largest group of non durable antistats. The most widely used are ditallowdimethylammonium chloride and dehydrogenated tallowdimethylammonium chloride.

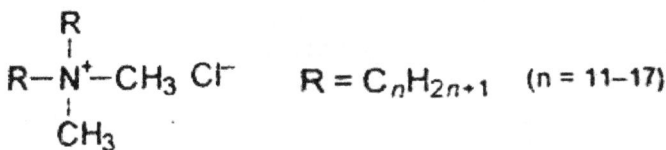

$$\overset{\overset{\textstyle R}{|}}{\underset{\underset{\textstyle CH_3}{|}}{R-N^+-CH_3}}\ Cl^- \qquad R = C_nH_{2n+1} \quad (n = 11\text{-}17)$$

Quaternary ammonium antistats

These are common ingredients in laundry and dryer applied consumer softeners. Like many other cationic antistats have an affinity for textile fibers and can be applied by exhaustion processes.

3. The last group of non-durable antistats is composed of non-ionic compounds such as ethoxylated fatty esters, alcohol and alkyl amines.

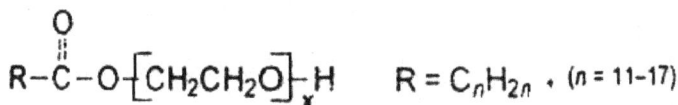

$$R-\overset{\overset{\textstyle O}{\|}}{C}-O-\!\!\left[CH_2CH_2O\right]_x\!\!-H \qquad R = C_nH_{2n} \cdot (n = 11\text{-}17)$$

Non-ionic antistats

Mixtures of cationic and non-ionic surfactants demonstrate synergistic antistatic properties. Non ionic materials provide increased moisture absorption and the cationic products provide the mobile counter ions.

3.5.2. Durable Antistatic

Obtaining antistatic properties that are durable to repeated launderings from a single finish application is difficult to achieve.

❖ The basic principle is to form a cross linked polymer network containing hydrophilic groups. Typically, polyamines are reacted with polyglycols to make such structures. These polymers can be formed prior to application to fabrics, or they can be formed in situ on the fiber surface after pad application.

❖ A variety of cross linking approaches can be used. One based on polyepoxides is shown below

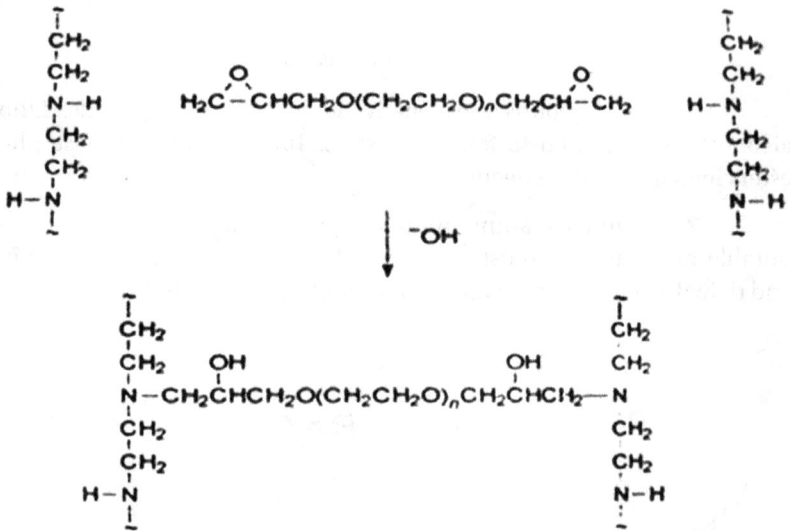

$$
\begin{array}{ccc}
\overset{|}{CH_2} & & \overset{|}{CH_2}\\
CH_2 & \overset{O}{\overset{\diagup\!\diagdown}{H_2C-CHCH_2O(CH_2CH_2O)_nCH_2CH-CH_2}} \;\;\overset{O}{\overset{\diagup\!\diagdown}{}} & CH_2\\
N-H & & H-N\\
CH_2 & & CH_2\\
CH_2 & & CH_2\\
H-N & & N-H
\end{array}
$$

$$\big\downarrow\; {}^-OH$$

$$
\begin{array}{cc}
\overset{|}{CH_2} & \overset{|}{CH_2}\\
CH_2\;\;\;\;OH & \;\;\;\;OH\;\;\;\;CH_2\\
N-CH_2CHCH_2O(CH_2CH_2O)_nCH_2CHCH_2-N\\
CH_2 & CH_2\\
CH_2 & CH_2\\
H-N & N-H
\end{array}
$$

Crosslinking of polyamines to form durable antistats

❖ The amount of hydrophilic character in the final polymer can be varied to meet individual requirements. The larger the hydrophilic portions, the more moisture are absorbed and the greater the antistatic effects obtained.

❖ However, at high levels of absorbed moisture, the polymer surface film softens and is more easily removed by abrasion during laundering. Higher degrees of cross linking will reduce the moisture absorption and subsequent swelling, but the antistatic effectiveness decreases.

❖ Additional difficulties with cross linked hydrophilic polymers include interferences with soil release and soil redeposition properties.

❖ Owing to the difficulties in achieving the perfect balance of desired properties, the use of durable antistatic finishes is limited.

❖ Other wash-fast antistatic agents are described in the literature, including polyhydroxypolyamines (PHPA) or polyalkylene and polyacrylic copolymers.

3.5.3. Mechanism of Antistatic Finishes

The principle mechanisms of antistatic finishes are increasing the conductivity of fiber surface (equivalent to lowering the surface resistivity) and reducing frictional forces through lubrication. The surface resistivity is defined as a 'material property of a substance whose numerical value is equal to the ratio of the voltage gradient to the current density. The resistivity is in effect the resistance of the fiber to electrical flow. Increasing conductivity produces a lower charge buildup and a more rapid dissipation while increased lubricity decreases the initial charge buildup. Antistatic agents that increase fiber surface conductivity form an intermediate layer on the surface. This layer is typically hygroscopic. The increased moisture content leads to higher conductivity. The presence of mobile ions on the surface is very important for increased conductivity. The effectiveness of hygroscopic antistatic finishes depends greatly on the humidity of the surrounding air during actual use; lower humidity leads to lower conductivity (higher resistance) and greater problems with static electricity. Most non-polymeric antistatic finishes are also surfactants that can orient themselves in specific ways at fiber surfaces. The hydrophobic structure parts of the molecule acts as lubricants to reduce charge buildup. This is particularly true with cationic antistatic surfactants that align with the hydrophobic group away from the fiber surface, similar to cationic softeners. The main antistatic effect from anionic and non ionic surfactants is increased conductivity from mobile ions and the hydration layer that surrounds the hydrophilic portion of the molecule since the surface orientation for these materials places the hydrated layer at the air interface.

3.6. Soil Release Finishes

The finish that allow stains to leave the fabric faster & makes fabric cleanable without significant loss of soil release properties. Soil release is the term used to describe the clean ability of the fabric by the laundring process.

3.6.1. Soiling

Soiling can be defined as smearing large surface of the fabric with dust or dirt or oil or grease or both.

3.6.2. Release Finish

Release finish allows stains to be removed more easily during laundering compare to most common untreated fabrics.

3.6.3. Mechanism of Soiling:

A fabric gets soiled mainly by three types of mechanism

By mechanical adhesion:

❖ The soil is adhere to the cloth by direct contact with a soiled surface or by rubbing of the garments against the skin or picking up dirt from liquors or from air.

❖ The fabric construction facilitates such adhesion as the soil gets entrapped in inter fiber and inter yarn spaces or even into the capillary spaces of the fiber where it gets firmly deposited. Also soil which is oily in nature can diffuse into the fiber.

By adhesion by electrical forces

❖ The soil is adhere to the fabric due to attraction of dust particles from air by electrically charged fiber surface.

❖ This phenomenon occurs mainly with synthetic fibers because of their low moisture regain. Positively charged fabric surface is soiled more than negatively charged surface.

By Re-deposition of soil during washing

Which occurs particularly with nylon and polyester fabrics,the redeposition on these

❖ Fibers takes place because of their oleophilic nature.

❖ Another aspect of soiling is the effect of time lag between soiling and washing. When a soiled fabric is allowed to lie unwashed for many days, the soil diffuses inside the fiber and it becomes difficult to remove it.

3.6.4. Factors Influencing Soiling

Moisture Regain

❖ Moisture regain of the fiber is the most important factor that influences soiling. Natural fibers and regenerated cellulose rayons have high moisture regain and have little tendency to accumulate static electricity. Even if static electricity is generated, it is quickly dissipated to the atmosphere.

❖ Therefore, the problem of soiling and soil removal is not very acute in the case of fibers having high moisture regain.

❖ Synthetic fibers have low moisture regain, therefore they accumulate static electricity which attracts dirt and dust from atmosphere.

❖ Lower the moisture regain, higher is the attraction of soil. When the moisture regain of the fibers drops below 4%, soiling increases rapidly.

❖ Polyester has the lowest moisture regain (0.4%) among synthetic fibers; therefore it attracts maximum soil. Since these fibers are hydrophobic, they do not swell in water and the removal of soil from the fiber becomes difficult.

❖ In the case of blends with cellulosic fibers, whatever soil is removed from the cellulosic component during washing, gets redeposited on the synthetic fiber because the synthetic fiber being oleophilic, attracts oily matter from the dirty wash waters.

Electrostatic Charge

❖ Synthetic fibers accumulate static charge during manufacture and during wear. Charged fibers attract soil from the atmosphere, positively charged fabric attracting more soil than the negatively charged one.

Fabric Construction

❖ Fabric construction, yarn count, twist and the cross section of the fiber influence soiling. Smaller the denier, greater is the tendency to soil because circular cross sectional fiber retains less soil than one with an irregular cross section

❖ Higher the twist in the yarn, greater the soil retention. Because Fabric with protruding fibers assists soiling.

❖ Loosely woven and open knitted fabrics are more prone to soiling than closely woven fabrics but removal of soil from loosely woven fabrics is easy. Because Fabrics made from filament yarn do not get soiled as fast as those made from spun yarns.

Particle Size of Soil

The smaller the size of the soil particles, grater is the soil retention by the fabric.

Mechanical Work Lead in Soil Release Finish

1. Hydrodynamic flow of washing washing carrying away the removed soil
2. Fiber flexing to force soil from between fibers during washing
3. Surface abrasion to remove soil physically during washing
4. Swelling of finish to reduce inter-fiber spacing.

3.6.5. Mechanism of Soil Release Finish (DUALACTION)

1. The flouro carbon polymers have the unusual property of being hydrophobic and oleophobic in air and hydrophilic and oil-releasing during the laundering process
2. This is called as dual action mechanism .
3. The hydrophilic blocks are shielded by the fluorocarbon segments when dry, presenting a repellent surface
4. After immersion in the wash bath, the hydrophilic blocks can swell and actually reverse the interfacial characteristics of the surface, yielding the hydrophilic surface necessary for easy oily soil release during washing.
5. So the detergent used during washing can easily penetrate inside the fabric and enhance the soil release.
6. Typically, these modified fluoro polymers are pad applied to fabrics followed by drying & curing

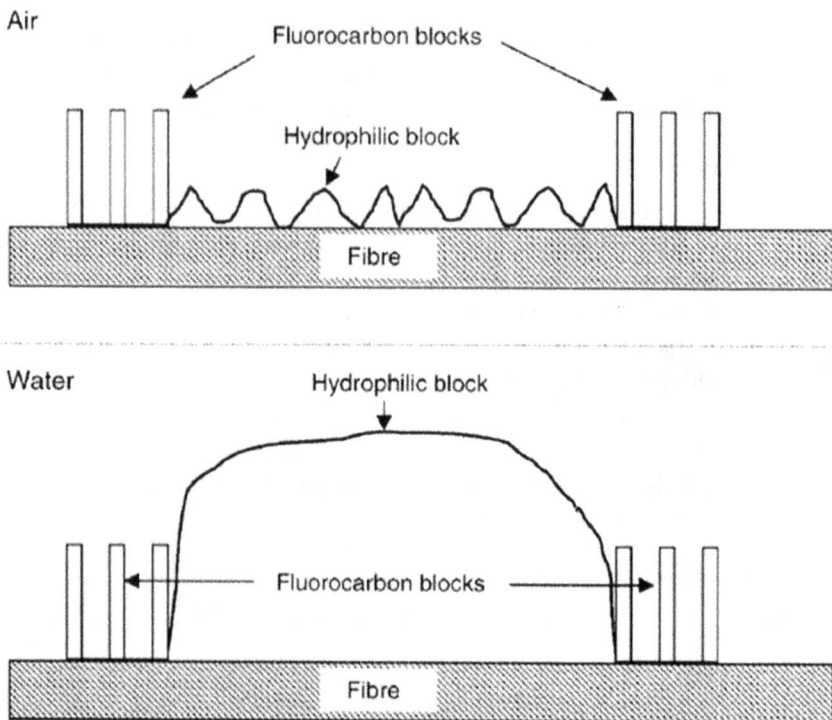

3.6.6. Factor Affecting the Soil Release Finish:

Factors	Explanation
Nature of the soil	Oily soil or particulate soil, hydrophobic or hydrophilic, liquid or solil
Kind of fibres	Type of fibre, hydrophilic or hydrophobic, smooth or porous fibre surface
Nature of textile	Textile construction; yarn (staple or filament), fabric (knit, woven or nonwoven
Effects of dyeing and printing	Difference in binder films, residual hydrophobic dyeing auxiliaries
Effects of other finishes	Compatible with antistatic finishes, easy-care finishes and other finishes not harmed by a hydrophilic surface.
	Not compatible with conventional repellent finishes and other finishes where hydrophilicity is detrimental to finish performance
Washing conditions	Detergents, hydrodynamic flow in the washing machine

3.6.7. Development in Soil Release Finishes

1. Stain-repellency performance has been achieved by the fluorocarbon resins based upon C8 perfluoroacrylates.

2. C8 fluorocarbon finishes produced via electrochemical fluorination, it is discontinued because PFOS (perfluorooctane sulfonate) can result as a breakdown product during the manufacturing process.

3. At present only C6 fluorocarbon products are manufactured using this route because they do not involve PFOS, which is a does not causes pollution that is also bioaccumulative.

3.6.8. Troubleshooting for Soil-release Finishes

1. The performance of a soil-release finish depends upon its ability to provide a hydrophilic surface during the laundering process.

2. Therefore any material deposited on the fibre surface that would reduce this necessary hydrophilicity should be avoided.

3. Softeners, lubricants and other products that modify surface properties should be carefully investigated in laboratory trials before being used with fabrics treated with soil-release finishes.

3.6.9. Properties Achieved by Soil Release

1. Add care to garments
2. Permits better wearability for improved soil release.
3. Provides greater comfort in hot weather.
4. Resists redepositing of soil when laundering.

3.6.10. Raising or Napping

A finishing process that raises the surface fibers of a fabric by means of passage over rapidly revolving cylinders covered with metal points or teasel burrs. Outing, flannel, and wool broadcloth derive their downy appearance from this finishing process. Napping is also used for certain knit goods, blankets, and other fabrics with a raised surface. This operation is particularly suitable for wool and cotton fabrics; it gives a fuzzy surface by abrading the cloth and pulling the fibre end to the surface. During those last years this process has also been applied on polyester/viscose blends and acrylic fabrics.

By means of this process a hairy surface can be given to both face and back of the cloth providing several modifications of the fabric appearance, softer and fuller hand and bulk increase. This enhances the resistance of the textile material to atmospheric agents, by improving thermal insulation and warmth provided by the insulating air cells in the nap. The fuzzy surface is created by pulling the fibre end out of the yarns by means of metal needles provided with hooks shelled into the rollers that scrape the fabric surface. The ends of the needles protruding from the rollers are 45°-hooks; their thickness and length can vary and they are fitted in a special rubber belt spiral-wound on the raising rollers. These rollers are generally alternated with a roller with hooks directed toward the fabric feed direction (pile roller), and a roller with the hooks fitted in the opposite direction (counterpile roller).

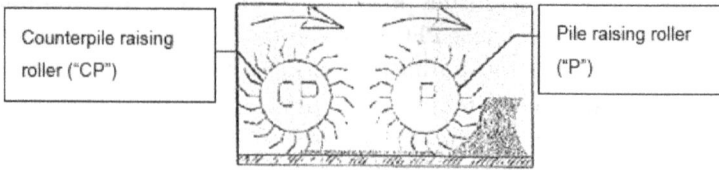

Raising rollers

The machine also includes some rotating brushes, which suction-clean the nibs in pile and counterpile directions. Actually the trend goes towards a ratio of raising rollers/pile rollers equal or 1/3. The two series of rollers have independent motion and can rotate with different speed and direction thus carrying out different effects.

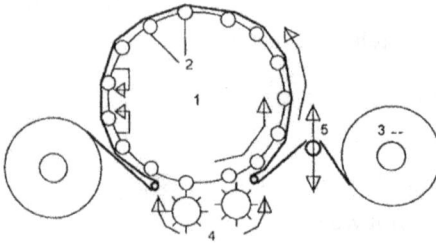

5. roller
6. rollers equipped with hooks
7. fabric
8. nib cleaning brushes
9. fabric tension adjustment

Raising (napping) machine

The action of these systems is almost powerful and the results depend upon the effects and the type of fabric desired . The raising effect can be obtained by adjusting the fabric tension (5) or by adjusting the speed and the roller rotation direction. Once a certain limit has been exceeded, the excessive mechanical stress could damage the fabric: it is therefore better, when carrying out a powerful raising, to pass the wet fabric through the raising machine many times (dry when processing cotton fabrics) and treat the fabrics in advance with softening-lubricating agents.

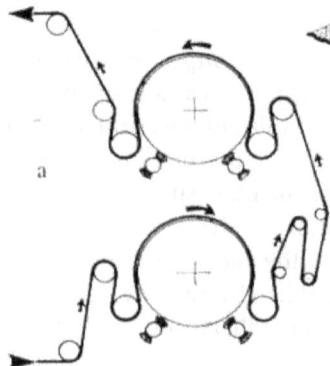

Raising the face of the fabric

The pile extraction is easier when carried out on single fibres: it is therefore suitable to reduce the friction between the fibres by wetting the material or, in case of cellulose fibres, by previously steaming the fabric. For the same reasons, it is better to use slightly twisted yarns.

The same machine allows different options of independent motions:

1. Fabric moving between entry and exit
2. Motion of large drum
3. Motion of raising rollers

The raising intensity can be adjusted by suitably combining the above mentioned independent motions, the tension of the textile material, the number of .pilewise. or . counterpile. raising rollers and their relative speed. It is possible to obtain .combed pile. raising effect, semi-felting effect with fibres pulled out and re-entered in the fabric, and complete felting effect. The raising machine is equipped with two overlapping drums each one featuring 24 rollers, which can process two faces or face and back of the same fabric. The drums assembled on a standard machine can rotate separately one from the other in the fabric feeding direction or in the opposite direction by carrying out a counter rotation. In this model all the functions are carefully monitored and controlled by a computer system; in particular all the commands are driven by alternating power motors controlled by Sensorless vector inverters.

The control electric system features

❖ PLC programmable controller for machine and alarms automation;
❖ Touch screen to program and update all processing parameters;
❖ Operating conditions of each single raising process (up to one million. recipes) that can be stored to facilitate the batch reproduction.

Furthermore, a series of special pressure rollers can be assembled on the feeding cylinders to prevent the fabric from sliding, thus granting an extremely smooth raising. The raising process ability lies merely in raising the desired quantity of fibre ends without excessively reducing the fabric resistance. For this reason, the technique applying the alternated use of pile and counterpile rollers is the most widely used since it minimises the loss of fibres from the fabric and the consequent resistance reduction. Standard raising machines have been designed to work with fabrics powerfully tensioned essentially because they are not equipped with an efficient and reliable tension control.

This gives rise to the effects detailed below

1. The contact surface between the fabric and the raising cylinders is quite small;
2. The hook nibs work only superficially on the fabric and the raising effect is quite reduced;
3. The fabric width is drastically reduced.

The above mentioned inconveniences have now been eliminated thanks to the last generation of raising machines, which reduce the number of passages and carry out the raising process by gently tensioning the fabric.

4   Special Purpose Finishes

4.1. Silicone finishes

Growth of silicones particularly in textiles has been enormous over the last few decades as it imparts particular hand along with flexibility, drapability, compressibility and elastic recovery to the textile fabrics. Softening and water-repellency are almost synonymous with silicone finishing in textiles. Advancement in science and technology has thoroughly engineered the basic structure of silicones to have series of functionally modified silicones which include the family of amino, carboxy and epoxy modified silicones. This paper reviews the fundamental aspects of silicone finishing in terms of structure property relationships. It also highlights on silicones for multifunctional finishing, micro/ macro/ nano finishing and water repellent finishing.

Keeping the colors, design and price of a garment or fabric aside, what ultimately a customer generally considers to choose a particular textile product in a retail shop is the handle and appearance of a garment. Practically everyone who examines a textile automatically touches it with their fingers to get an impression of the hand. Hence, almost all apparel and home furnishing textiles are treated with softeners. Only a few specialty fabrics do not receive a softener finish, consequently, it is easier to state which fabrics are not softened. These include wall coverings, carpeting and most industrial textiles. Therefore, softening of textiles becomes an important finishing process of many after treatment processes in a textile chemical processing industry. The hand of a fabric is a subjective sensation felt by the skin when a textile fabric is touched with the finger tips and gently compressed. e perceived softness of a textile is the combination of several measurable physical phenomena such as elasticity, compressibility and smoothness.

Almost all the natural fibres, by providence arrangement, have some percentage of wax which makes fibre naturally soft, the classical example is cotton, the most widely used fibre. However, the presence of wax both on the surface and on the bulk of fibre makes it resistant for wetting. Unfortunately, the lack of water absorbency makes the fibres unsuitable for dyeing and printing which are the primary objectives of a textile processing unit. Therefore, in order to make the fibre suitable for dyeing, various preparatory processes such as desizing, scouring, bleaching, *etc.* are carried out, which actually remove the natural softening agents to make the fibres more absorbent. Therefore, generally after dyeing and printing the fabrics become harsh and stiff. Finishing with softeners can overcome this deficiency and even improve on the original suppleness. The softening treatments impart soft handle (supple, pliant, sleek and fluffy), smoothness and enhance flexibility, drape and pliability. Other properties improved by softeners include the feeling of added fullness, antistatic properties and sew ability.

With chemical softeners, textiles can achieve an agreeable, soft hand and some smoothness. However, the disadvantages sometimes seen with chemical softeners include reduced crock fastness, yellowing of white goods, changes in hue of dyed goods and fabric structure slippage. Most softeners consist of molecules with both a hydrophobic and a hydrophilic part. Therefore, they can be classified as surfactants (surface active agents) and are to be found concentrated at the fibre surfaces. Most softeners have low water solubility. Therefore softening products are usually sold as oil in water emulsions containing 20-30% solids. The softener molecules typically contain a long alkyl group, sometimes branched, of more than 16 and up to 22 carbon atoms, but most have 18 corresponding to the stearyl residue. Exceptions to this molecular structure are the special categories of silicones, paraffins and polyethylene softeners. About one-third of the softeners used in the textile industry are silicone based as it imparts excellent soft hand combined with various other properties such as water repellency, superior smoothness, greasy feel, excellent body, improved crease resistance, *etc.* The silicones were actually first utilized by the textile industry primarily as lubricants in fibre and fabric manufacture. Silicone softeners are also applied with permanent press finishes to improve garment wear life and permanent press finish durability. It can also be used with other finishing agents for multifunctional finishes, for example, it can be used in resin finishing of textiles to have a soft wrinkle resistant fabric. Recently, by Americos Industries, silicone softeners are also formulated with special polymers to impart a unique leather soft finish. This article, therefore, discusses the fundamental principles behind silicone finishing, various developments in silicones and their corresponding textile applications. This paper includes the contribution from Americos in the field of silicone finishing of textiles.

4.1.1. Silicones

In the science of silicone finishing, a fundamental difference between silicon and silicone should be noted, in that silicon is an atom that lies below carbon atom in the periodic table, while the term silicone refers to artificial polymers based on a framework of altering silicon and oxygen (siloxane bonds). The electronic configuration of silicon is $1S^2, 2S^2, 2P^6, 3S^2, 3P^2$. The larger atomic radius of silicon atom makes the silicon-silicon single bond much less energetic due to which the silanes

$(Si_nH_{2n} + _1)$ are much less stable than alkanes. The opposite, however, is true of silicon-oxygen bonds that are more energetic (about 22 Kcal/ mole) than the carbon oxygen bonds. Polysiloxanes, therefore, have recurring Si-O linkages in the backbones.

4.1.2. Silanes Vs Polysiloxanes

Generally, the silicone treatment of textile consists of treating them with silicone polymer emulsions but not with the silane monomers which may also impart the softness and water repellent characteristics. The reason being is that the silane monomers, during treatment, liberate hazardous chemicals, for instance treatment of textiles with chloromethylsilanes liberates hydrochloric acid. Attempts have been made to improve the treatment of textiles with silane monomers, using of ammonia to absorb the hydrochloric acid in the case of chloromethylsilanes. The attempts which have been patented are replacement of chlorine with acetoxy, alkoxy, amino, or isocyanate groups. However, none of these has resulted in a practical process. Therefore, silanes are not used as such for textile finishing but are converted to polysiloxanes, which can be applied to textiles as solutions in organic solvents or as aqueous emulsions.

4.1.3. Polysiloxanes

The chemistry and technology of polysiloxanes have been the interest of many researchers and manufacturers as it finds very wide applications, the silicones used for textile applications are polymers with a -O-Si-O- backbone. According to proper chemical nomenclature, these polymers are polysiloxanes

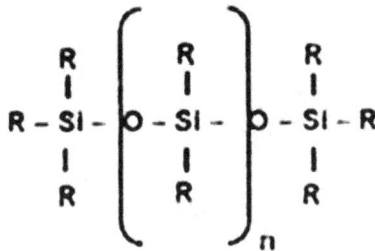

$$R - \underset{\underset{R}{\overset{\overset{R}{|}}{|}}}{Si} - \left[O - \underset{\underset{R}{\overset{\overset{R}{|}}{|}}}{Si} - \right]_n O - \underset{\underset{R}{\overset{\overset{R}{|}}{|}}}{Si} - R$$

Polysiloxane

Engineering of silicone oxygen of siloxane bonds (fig. 1) with organic substitutes results in various kinds silicone polymers [6]. Accordingly, the substituents R can be a hydrogen, hydroxyl, alkyl, aryl, or alkoxyl group. The substituents in the polymer chain can be all of the same kind or can be different. However, for textile applications, R is usually either methyl or hydrogen groups and are the most important of the organic substituents used in commercial silicones, the vast majorities of which are polydimethylsiloxanes (PMDS). Polysiloxane is a mixture of inorganic and organic substances. Because of their inorganic-organic structure and the flexibility of the siloxane bonds, silicones have the following unique properties,

❖ Thermal/ oxidative stability,

❖ Low temperature flow ability,

❖ Low viscosity change with temperature,

❖ High compressibility,

❖ Low surface tension (spreadability), and

❖ Low fire hazard

They also have good electrical insulating (dielectric properties) characteristics and water repellency (hydrophobicity) which are maintained over a wide range of temperatures. As a result of having combined unique properties, these semi-inorganic materials i.e. polysiloxanes become industrially important and find applications in many diverse markets, such as aerospace, automotive, construction, electrical, electronics, medical materials, performance chemicals and coatings, personal care and textiles . Fluids and greases, emulsions, rubber products and resins are some of the materials based on silicone technology.

4.1.4. Textile applications

Silicones have broad utility in textile processing and finishing; most of the products for this industry are based on PMDS technology. The applications for silicones vary widely and include antifoam for fabric and carpet dyeing, print paste softeners, fabric finishes and coatings. In fabric processing, silicone antifoams are often used to maximize the efficiency of the scouring baths, washing/dyeing and bleaching options. They serve as fibre lubricants for spinning, winding and slashing. Various types of silicones are commonly used as softeners, wetting agents and water repellents. In sewing operations, silicone thread lubricants are essential to meet the demands of industrial high-speed sewing machinery. Silicones also have many uses in nonwoven applications such as binders, additives for wet-laid processes. Some silicones are supplied as neat fluids, while others are in the form of emulsions or room temperature curing elastomers. PMDS is extremely versatile, and can be modified to formulate a wide range of products with tailored hydrophobicity and durability, used to modify the feel and appearance of fabrics, or to improve processing.

4.1.4.1 Type: durable and nondurable / reactivity

Aminosilicones are for durable finish. Polydimethylsiloxane is a non durable finish [11]. Polydimethylsiloxane with its terminal reactive hydroxyl groups is a conventional, may be semi-durable finish. Polymethylhydrogensiloxanes acts as a reactive as well as cross-linking agent and hence is responsible for producing durable finish with the blend of polydimethylsiloxane. Aminofunctional silicones and other organo-functional silicones contain groups such as amino, substituted amino, epoxide, or alcohol groups attached to the polymer backbone. Therefore, they offer durable, soft and lively hand and a slight increase in wrinkle recovery and flat appearance. The presence of silane coupling also plays a major role in enhancing the durability .Silicone softeners include both polydimethylsiloxane polymers as well as a wide range of organo-modified polydimethylsiloxanes. Performance enhancing additives and finishes based on PMDS technology can be nonreactive, conventional reactive or the organo-functional materials. With these silicones, one of the advantage to the processors is that the ability to derive mort~ than one benefit from a single product.

Organo-modified polydimethylsiloxanes, particularly epoxy modified, were found to offer a significant improvement over conventional unreactive silicones. The improvement was in terms of both a greater degree of softening and good durability of polymers to laundering. Amino-functional polydimethylsiloxanes softeners were found to have the same advantages as reactive silicones. Two additional benefits were found with aminofunctional silicone softeners. Knit fabrics became more elastic, with better stretch recovery.

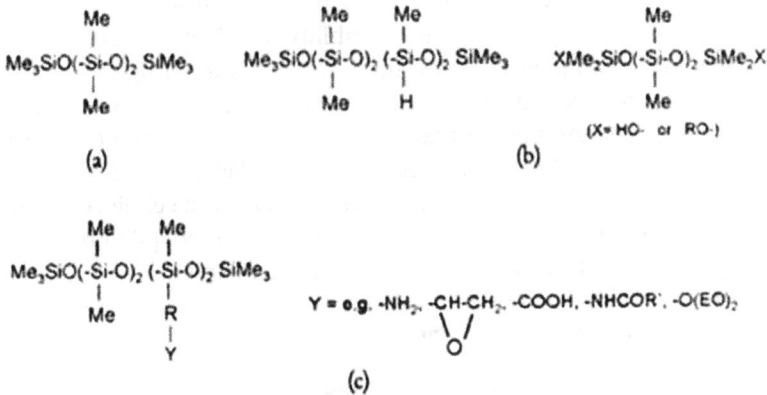

$$
\begin{array}{ccc}
\text{Me} & \text{Me} \quad \text{Me} & \text{Me} \\
| & | \quad\quad | & | \\
\text{Me}_3\text{SiO(-Si-O)}_2\,\text{SiMe}_3 & \text{Me}_3\text{SiO(-Si-O)}_2\,(\text{-Si-O})_2\,\text{SiMe}_3 & \text{XMe}_2\text{SiO(-Si-O)}_2\,\text{SiMe}_2\text{X} \\
| & | \quad\quad | & | \\
\text{Me} & \text{Me} \quad\, \text{H} & \text{Me} \\
& & (\text{X= HO- or RO-}) \\
\text{(a)} & \text{(b)} &
\end{array}
$$

$$
\begin{array}{l}
\text{Me} \quad \text{Me} \\
| \quad\quad | \\
\text{Me}_3\text{SiO(-Si-O)}_2\,(\text{-Si-O})_2\,\text{SiMe}_3 \\
| \quad\quad | \\
\text{Me} \quad \text{R} \\
\quad\quad\quad | \\
\quad\quad\quad \text{Y}
\end{array}
\qquad
\text{Y = e.g. -NH}_2,\ \text{-CH-CH}_2,\ \text{-COOH, -NHCOR', -O(EO)}_2
$$

$$
\text{-CH-CH}_2 \ \text{(epoxide, O)}
$$

(c)

Example of a) nonreactive silicone polymer b) conventionally reactive silicone polymer c) organofunctional reactive silicone polymer

The softener also additionally delivered antistatic benefits and wrinkling resistance. These two benefits and the fact that the amino functional silicone are readily adsorbed from dilute solutions onto cotton fabrics in conjunction with traditional cationic softeners lead to their use in rinse cycle softeners in the middle to late 1980s. One of the features shared by many silicone materials is effectiveness at very low concentrations. Very small amounts (0.1 to 1.0% by weight) are usually required to achieve the desired properties, which can improve the cost efficiency of textile operations and help ensure a minimum of environmental impact. Therefore, in spite of high cost, amine silicones did bring a consumer-perceptible new dimension to rinse cycle fabric softeners. The reactivity of polydimethylsiloxanes can be increased by mixing with polymethylhydrogensiloxanes. The Si-H bond is hydrolyzed to -Si-OH, which can condense with another Si-OH group or a -Si-H group and forms cross links. However, hydrolysis produces hydrogen, which may create a fire hazard and a storage problem.

The Si-H bond hydrolyzes rapidly in an alkaline or strongly acidic medium but can be stabilized with certain organic additives in an aqueous medium buffered at pH 3-4. Oxidation of -Si-H groups by atmospheric oxygen or oxidizing agents can produce -SiOH groups, which can also contribute to eventual cross-linking of the finish on the fabric. Polymethylhydrogensiloxanes produce a hard brittle film on fibres and the finish has a harsh handle. They are, therefore, not used alone, but in admixture with polydimethylsiloxanes, which act as plasticizers and improve the handle of the finished fabric. However polymethylhydrogen siloxanes can produce a highly water-repellent finish with a soft handle when crosslinked on cotton in the presence of organic peroxides.

The water repellency of silicones on synthetic fabrics, especially those made of filament fibres, is fairly resistant to laundering and dry-cleaning with pure solvents. The loss of water repellency during dry cleaning is caused mainly by adsorption of hydrophilic substances, such as detergents, and to a lesser extent by dissolution of the silicone finish in the solvent. The durability of silicone finishes on cellulosic fabric is impaired by swelling of cotton fibres during laundering. The expansion of the fibres ruptures the silicone film essential for water repellency. Since the repellent polysiloxane film does not melt and flow, the cracks in the ruptured film cannot be sealed and the initial repellency restored by heating. Although attempts have been made to form a covalent bond between the polysiloxane and cellulose fibres, the -Si-O-CELL bond is yet not stable to hydrolysis. Apart from the type of reactive groups, the viscosity and the adsorption mechanism of the softener, as well as treatment conditions such as curing temperature, are crucial factors affecting the performance properties of the treated fabrics.

4.1.4.2 Method of preparation of silicones

The hydrophobicity of silicones was discovered at General Electric by Patnode, who observed that paper treated with chloromethylsilanes become water repellent when exposed to moist air. Preparations of such substituted chlorosilanes R_n- $SiCL_{4-n}$ where R is usually a methyl or phenyl group and n = 0, 1, 2, or 3 is the first step in the manufacture of silicones. There are two methods available for the preparation of chlorosilanes. In the first, direct process, the starting materials can be prepared through hydrolyses of alkyl or arylsilicone halides. Organosilicone halides, in turn, are made commercially by heating alkyl or aryl halides with silicone at 250 to 289°C. Copper catalyzes this reaction. The second method is the Grignard method in which a given chlorosilanes or a mixture is reacted with methyl or phenyl magnesium halide to yield the desired more highly alkylated or arylated chlorosilanes. Neither of the above methods of synthesis yields any given chlorosilanes free from the other members of its series. For example chloromethylsilanes are hydrolyzed by water to silanols, which condense spontaneously to siloxanes. Chlorotrimethylsilane yields hexamethyldisiloxane.

$$RCl + Si \xrightarrow[Cu]{250 - 280°C} SiCl_4 + RSiCl_3 + R_2SiCl_2 + R_3SiCl$$

The same materials can also be formed by the Grignard reaction:

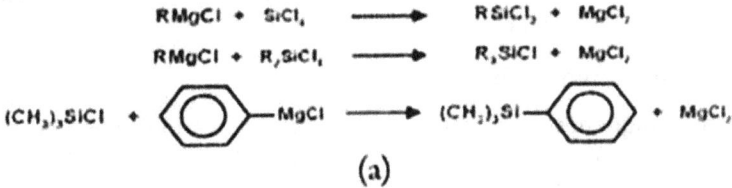

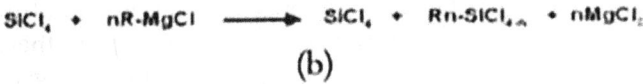

$$RMgCl + SiCl_4 \longrightarrow RSiCl_3 + MgCl_2$$

$$RMgCl + R_2SiCl_2 \longrightarrow R_3SiCl + MgCl_2$$

$$(CH_3)_3SiCl + \langle\bigcirc\rangle{-}MgCl \longrightarrow (CH_3)_3Si{-}\langle\bigcirc\rangle + MgCl_2$$

(a)

$$SiCl_4 + nR{-}MgCl \longrightarrow SiCl_4 + Rn{-}SiCl_{4-n} + nMgCl_2$$

(b)

Preparation of chlorosilanes a) first method b) second method

Dichlorodimethylsilane yields, depending on reaction conditions, 20 - 50% cyclic siloxanes and 80 - 50% linear polydimethylsiloxanes. Trichloromethylsilane yields cross-linked polymethylsiloxanes. Condensation reactions can occur between -SiOH and -SiH groups, if present, and between two -SiOH groups. In the presence of peroxides or upon irradiation, two -$SiCH_3$ groups can also undergo a condensation reaction. The hydrolysis and condensation reactions of chloromethylsilanes or chlorohydrogensilanes are, therefore, more complex than those shown above and hence the separation of the reaction products requires highly efficient fractional distillation columns - a difficult processing step in the manufacture of silicone

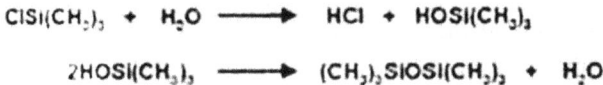

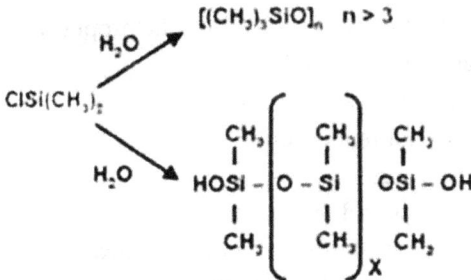

$$ClSi(CH_3)_3 + H_2O \longrightarrow HCl + HOSi(CH_3)_3$$

$$2HOSi(CH_3)_3 \longrightarrow (CH_3)_3SiOSi(CH_3)_3 + H_2O$$

$$[(CH_3)_2SiO]_n \quad n > 3$$

$$ClSi(CH_3)_2 \nearrow^{H_2O}$$

$$\searrow_{H_2O}$$

$$HOSi \begin{matrix} CH_3 \\ | \\ \\ | \\ CH_3 \end{matrix} - \left(\begin{matrix} CH_3 \\ | \\ O - Si \\ | \\ CH_3 \end{matrix} \right)_x \begin{matrix} CH_3 \\ | \\ OSi - OH \\ | \\ CH_2 \end{matrix}$$

Hydrolyses of chloromethylsilanes

The polymerized silicones are prepared by hydrolyzing a known mixture of pure substituted chlorosilanes with water, washing the hydrolysate free from hydrochloric acid and further polymerizing the neutral hydrolysate to yield the desired product. The silicone fluids are prepared from mono - and difunctional chlorosilanes so as to get end-blocked linear polymers.

4.1.4.3 Silicone: for softening

As the uniqueness of silicone finishing has been established in the previous sections, this section expands further on silicones as softeners. As the soft touch, supple feel and appearance, *etc.* are of significantly important for a customer, softening of textiles has become an important finishing operation. Silicone emulsions, especially, are capable of bestowing significant benefits in this regard. Therefore, silicone softeners are becoming extremely important because of their very good softness and greater wash permanence compared to other softeners. The mechanism of softening by silicone treatment is due to flexible film formation. The reduced energy required for bond rotation makes the siloxane backbone more flexible. Therefore, polysiloxanes form a flexible film on fibres and yarns and hence reduces the interfibre and inter yarn friction. Thus the silicone finishing of textile produce an exceptional soft handle combined with other properties such as superior smoothness, greasy feel, excellent body, improved crease resistance, *etc.*

The silicone molecules can produce a wide range of hand variations, from dry to oily to resilient, and are also used for such purposes. The extent of the effect depends on the degree to which the molecules are cross linked. The responsibility from the finisher side is to select the appropriate silicone softener from the vast range available in the textile auxiliaries sector. Silicones particularly as softener are expected to confer the following.

- ❖ Soft supple hand
- ❖ Improved sewability
- ❖ Improved tear strength
- ❖ Improved crocking fastness
- ❖ Outstanding hydrophobic or hydrophilic properties
- ❖ Higher crease recovery angle
- ❖ Improved wash permanence
- ❖ Very good anti-pilling properties
- ❖ Antistatic properties
- ❖ High effectiveness and process stability

Silicone softeners include both polydimethylsiloxane polymers as well as a wide range of organo-modified pol ydimethylsiloxanes. Polydimethylsiloxanes, polymethylhydrogen-siloxanes or blend of these two fluids are generally used as softeners. Silicone softeners are also applied with permanent press finishes to improve garment wear life and permanent press finish durability. Organo-modified polydimethylsiloxanes, particularly epoxy modified, were found to offer a significant improvement over conventional unreactive silicones. The improvement was in terms of both a greater degree of softening and good durability of polymers to laundering. Of the silicone softeners available, perhaps the most common in current industrial usage and likely to be the best is the amino functional silicone softeners. These materials offer a range of handles depending on the relative size of x and the ratio of x:y. They may be supplied as surfactantstabilized emulsions in water, either mechanical or microemulsions. Mechanical emulsions contain large droplets which tend to coalesce on the fabric, giving surface effects. The microemulsions, of much smaller droplet size, will tend to migrate into the yarn and give an overall softness to the whole structure. The aminosilicones may give a relatively dry handle where the x:y ratio is high, and a typically greasy handle where the x:y ratio is low.

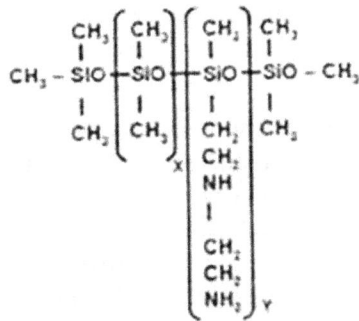

Aminofunctional softener

Aminofunctional silicone fluids are much more effective at imparting hand properties than either methyl oils or silicones with carboxyl or epoxy functions. This exceptional property stems from the fact that the partly protonated amino groups of the softener molecule interact with the negatively charged cotton fibres. Hence, the amino functional silicones are readily adsorbed from dilute solutions onto cotton fabrics in conjunction with traditional cationic organic softeners lead to their use in rinse cycle softeners. Two additional benefits were found with aminofunctional silicone softeners. Knit fabrics became more elastic, with better stretch recovery. The softener also additionally delivered antistatic benefits and wrinkling resistance. All these fabric property improvements exhibited durability to repeated launderings. In addition the ability to blend these aminofunctional silicones with organic softeners and retain performance properties allow the creation of softener blends with optimum cost - performance parameters. Thus a polyester cotton blend fabric showed improvement in durable press rating, wrinkle recovery and tear strength even when half the amino functional silicone softener was replaced by an organic softener, which however caused a loss in stretch/ recovery performance of cotton knit fabric after five washes.

Microemulsions are generally aminosilicones. Epoxy silicones can also be used as microemulsions but softness is not as good as amino-micro silicone emulsions.

Microsilicone emulsions give a permanent feel to the fabric with a high degree of softness [21]. Amino functional silicones have shown good softening ability. Increased tear strength, greater abrasion resistance and improved wrinkle recovery are seen on polyester cotton blends and 100% cotton woven fabrics treated with aminofunctional silicones along with a durable press resin.

4.1.5. Silicones for multifunctional finish

Since the curing conditions of the polysiloxanes are similar to durable press cross-linking treatments with methylol compounds, polysiloxanes can be applied with a durable press finish. The durable press resins enhance the durability of the silicone finish. Wrinkle free finishes are renowned for the substantial quantities of glyoxal crosslinker and catalysts employed. Since the finishing process occurs in an acid milieu, silicone softeners are expected to be stable in saline solution and acids, and to be resistant to 'shear. Not many silicone softeners on the market can meet these demands.

Americos is one of the leading manufacturers of softeners both silicones based and non-silicones based for various textile substrates to impart soft handle along with various other special properties. Particularly, Americos silicone softeners are engineered to impart multifunctional properties. For example, Americos FX-30 is silicone based softener specially engineered with polyurethane (PU) polymers for white fabrics. It imparts excellent and durable softness to the fabric along with a special supple feel due to the presence of PU polymers. In addition, it also enhances the whiteness of the treated fabric. Americos also has commercialized a range of multifunctional silicone softeners such as Americos Rubrisoft FL, Americos Leather Soft 750 and Americos Rabroxil5011 which are produced using unique silicone polymer and combination of special polymers. Americos Rubrisoft FL gives acme bouncy effect commonly understood as stretch or rubbery effect. The finish is durable and it improves wrinkle recovery property fabric significantly along with softening. Similarly Americos Leather Soft 750 and Americos Rabrom 5011 impart a bulky, soft hand and non yellowing leather like effect. They also provide protection against harmful UV-B rays. Further, they increase the strength significantly and improve crease recovery property.

4.1.5.1 Micro/macro/nano emulsions

There are vast differences between the conventional microemulsions that made history in the textiles industry around 20 years ago, and the quite recent generation of macroemulsions. The primary difference is the panicle size of the silicones. These may be up to 80 nm in microemulsions, whereas they are at least 120 nm in macroemulsions.

Microemulsions are generally easier to make, but they also have their disadvantages. Adding more of them produces only a very limited increase in their softening effect. As more is added, the resultant higher proportion of emulsifier leads to hand saturation and may even cause it to deteriorate. With macroemulsions, however, this effect if it occurs at all - only becomes noticeable at much higher application rates. Unlike microemulsions, macroemulsions provide more resilience, smoothness and a fuller hand. However, its mechanical application properties depend crucially on the quality of the macroemulsions. Poorly emulsified emulsions bring more disadvantages than advantages. To optimize the desired parameters, such as panicle size distribution, homogeneity and shear stability, the right processing technology is needed.

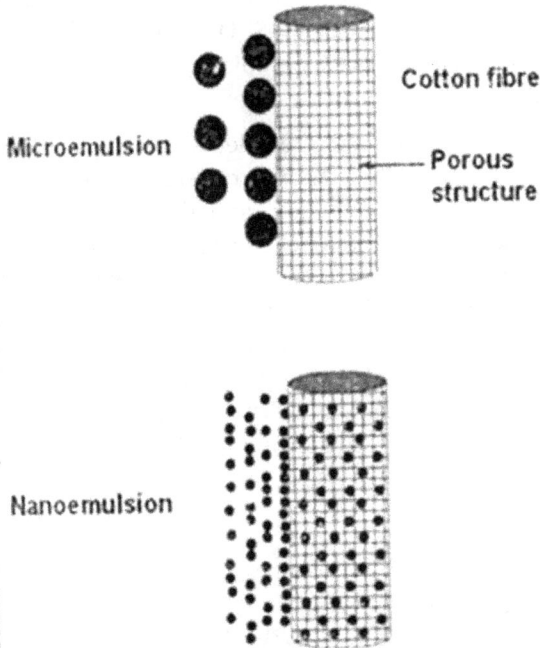

Schematic representation of diffusion of micro and nano silicone emulsion droplets in cotton fibre

With the help of extreme shear technology, Americos emerges out with silicone nanoemulsions which have their unique penetrability it; the fabric and fibre structure. Thus it results in excellent softening properties. The schematic diagram shown in figure 6 depicts the penetration of silicone nanoemulsion droplets inside the structure of cotton. The cotton fibre is made of fibrillar structure and hence it has porous structure. The droplet size of nanoemulsion is so small that it can penetrate the micro and nanostructures very well compared to the droplets of microemulsions. Therefore, using Americos nanoemulsions, it is possible to obtain special softening effect. Americos Nanosoft 1140, Americos Nanosoft 1180, Americos Nanosoft 950 I and Americos Nano soft 2000 are the various silicone nanoemulsions currently Americos sells in the market for various textiles. These silicone nanoemulsions impart durable softness, crease resistance, oily and greasy soft hand, suppleness and limpness, excellent body, superior smoothness, and surface levelness.

4.1.5.2 Silicone finishing and water repellency

In addition to imparting soft feeling, silicone finishing, in general, imparting water repellent property to the textiles. Such water repellency property is provided by methyl group which are oriented and attached to the fibre surface by silicone links. The silicones are mostly built up of polymethylhydrogen siloxane and polydimethyl siloxane. The first one is reactive and is generally used as water-repellent mostly along with the second one. The problem with the reactive low molecular weight polysiloxanes is that they are liable to undergo further polymerization by lengthening of the -Si-O- chain and also by crosslinking of adjacent -Si-O- chains. This is undesirable in textile application and is prevented by previously replacing the end hydrogen atoms by more inert substituents like methyl groups.

Advantages of silicone water repellents include a high degree of water repellency at relatively low (0.5 - 1 % owf) concentrations, very soft fabric hand, improved sewability and shape retention, and improved appearance and feel of pile fabrics. Some modified silicone repellents can be exhaust applied (to pressure-sensitive fabrics). However, some of the limitations with the silicone repellents are increased pilling and seam slippage, reduced repellency if excessive amounts are applied (for example silicone double layer with polar outside, only moderate durability to laundering (through hydrolysis of siloxane and rupture of the film by strong cellulose fibre swelling) and dry cleaning (adsorption of surfactants), and no oil and soil repellency. The silicone finish may enhance the attraction of hydrophobic dirt.

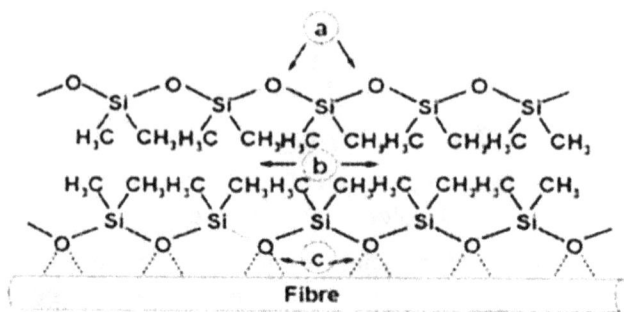

Silicone double layers on fibre, a) Polar
surface, b) Hydrophobic attraction of the methyl
groups, c) Hydrogen bonds to polar fibre surface

However, while silicone finishing is considered only for enhancing the fabric handle, the hydrophobic property imparted as a result of silicone finishing becomes a problem rather than to be an advantage. Attempts have been thus made to enhance the hydrophilicity of the silicone treated fabrics. Okada *et al.* have grafted acrylamide over the silicone treated surface in order to render it a hydrophilic property. The authors have first treated with corona discharge in air to introduce peroxides onto the surface. These peroxides were further used to graft the acrylamide. Likewise there are many attempts made to enhance the hydrophilicity of the silicone treated textiles. However, *Americos* with its special R&D efforts have discovered special silicone softeners which not only enhance fabric handle properties but also preserve the hydrophilicity. *Americos SF 1402* and *Amerisoft Sil HL- 40 AS* are the two special hydrophilic silicone softeners that are currently in the market. They impart very good hydrophilicity, durable softness and excellent shear stability. They are also compatible with cationic and nonionic softeners and are stable with resin applications.

4.1.5.3 Silicones containing amide groups: non-yellowing

One limitation with the aminofunctional silicone is that the amino group which is responsible for many unique properties also results in a propensity to yellowing, particularly during curing or drying, and the likelihood of yellowing increases with increasing amino content. Therefore, silicones containing not an amino group but an amide group were developed. The benefits of these softeners are that they are essentially nonyellowing, and that the handle is very dry when compared to even the low-amine aminosilicones.

When low-yellowing silicone softeners are needed, amino fluids with low amine number are generally preferred. They tend to be used for white goods and pale shades. The higher the amine number of the aminoethyl-aminopropyl fluid, the more yellowing can be expected.

Silicone softener
containing amide group

One corollary of this is that the hand becomes softer. Americos Silsoft 1140 and Americos Silky top are some of the prominent silicone softeners of which Americos Silkytop is a blend of cationic and silicone softener. It has especially nonyellowing character and it can be used for cotton, polyester and their blends. It imparts cotton garment excellent supple, soft and brilliant look. It does not affect dye fastness rather it increases the shade depth.

Silicone finishing is becoming increasingly important in textiles as it imparts a very unique soft handle with supple, pliant, sleek and fluffy effect. It also enhances smoothness, flexibility, drape and pliability of the fabric greatly. Manipulation of the basic silicone chemistry has resulted in multifunctional finishes that not only impart the unique soft hand of silicone but also the other essential properties such as crease resistance, wrinkle resistance, leather soft effect, durability *etc.* Silicone nanoemulsions, as it shows improved penetrability into the textile structures produces favorable unusual soft hand and other properties that are obtained with micro and macro emulsions. Americos has particularly shown its excellence in producing the silicone nanoemulsions and special silicone softeners for multifunctional finishes with its state-of-the-art manufacturing technology.

4.2. Denim finishes

A popular conception of the etymology of the word denim is that it is a contraction or derivative of the French term, serge de Nmes. Denim was traditionally colored blue with indigo dye to make blue jeans, though jean then denoted a different, lighter cotton textile; the contemporary use of jean comes from the French word for Genoa, Italy (Gnes), from which the first denim trousers were made. Records of a group of New Yorkers headed for the California gold fields in 1849 show that they took along four hickory shirts apiece. Hickory cloth would later furnish the material for some fatigue pantaloons and shirts in the American Civil War. Denim is a rugged cotton twill textile, in which the weft passes under two (*twi-* "double") or more warp fibers, producing the familiar diagonal ribbing identifiable on the reverse of the fabric.

4.2.1. Denim washing

Denim washing is the aesthetic finish given to the denim fabric to enhance the appeal and to provide strength. Dry denim, as opposed to washed denim, is a denim fabric that is not washed after being dyed during its production. Much of the appeal of dry denim lies in the fact that with time the fabric will fade in a manner similar to that which artificially distressed denim attempts to replicate. With dry denim, however, such fading is affected by the body of the person who wears the jeans and the activities of their daily life. This creates what many feel to be a more natural, unique look than pre-distressed denim.

Denim washes are of two types

1. Mechanical washes

- ❖ Stone wash
- ❖ Microsanding

2. Chemical washes

- ❖ Denim bleaching
- ❖ Enzyme wash
- ❖ Acid wash

4.2.2. Chemical wash

Denim bleach

❖ In this process a strong oxidative bleaching agent such as sodium hypochlorite or $KMnO_4$ is added during the washing with or without stone addition.

❖ Discoloration produced is usually more apparent depending on strength of the bleach liquor quantity, temperature and treatment time.

❖ It is preferable to have strong bleach with short treatment time.

❖ Care should be taken for the bleached goods so that they should be adequately antichlored or after washed with peroxide to minimize yellowing. Materials should be carefully sorted before processing for color uniformity.

Limitations:

– Process is difficult to control i.e. difficult to reach the same level of bleaching in repeated runs.

❖ When desired level of bleaching reached the time span available to stop the bleaching is very narrow. Due to harshness of chemical, it may cause damage to cellulose resulting in severe strength losses and/or breaks or pinholes at the seam, pocket, *etc.*

❖ Harmful to human health and causes corrosion to stainless steel.

❖ Required antichlor treatment.

❖ Problem of yellowing is very frequent due to residual chlorine.

❖ Chlorinated organic substances occur as abundant products in bleaching, and pass into the effluent where they cause severe environmental pollution.

4.2.3. Enzyme Wash

It is environmentally friendly wash. It involves the Application of organic enzymes that eat away at the fabric, i.e. the cellulose. When the desired color is achieved, the enzymes can be stopped by changing the alkalinity of the bath or its temperature. Post treatment includes final rinsing and softening cycle. The effects produced by the cellulose enzyme are,

1. Use of cellulase making the seams, hems, and pockets more noticeable

2. Salt pepper effect is color contrast effect.

3. Faded garment with acid cellulase enzyme provides less color contrast in proportion to garment washed with neutral cellulase enzymes. Garment load size of the machine is 35-40 jeans per machine and it cannot be overloaded.

4.2.4. Acid wash

It is done by tumbling the garments with pumice stones presoaked in a solution of sodium hypochlorite or potassium permanganate for localized bleaching resulting in a non uniform sharp blue/white contrast.

In this wash the color contrast of the denim fabric can be enhanced by optical brightening. The advantage of this process is that it saves water as addition of water is not required.

Process cycle

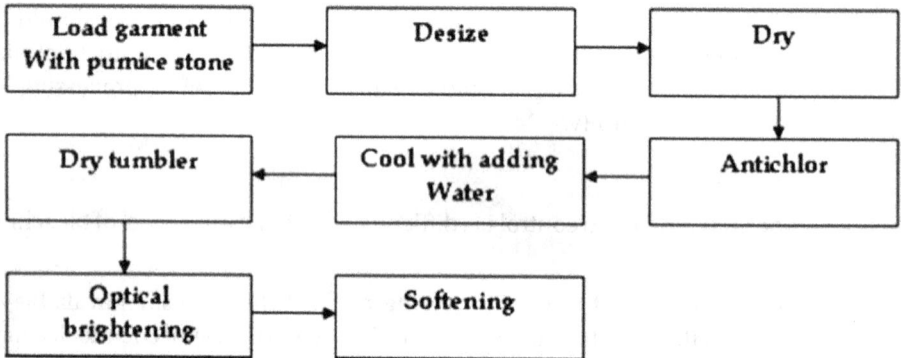

```
┌─────────────────┐      ┌─────────────────┐      ┌─────────────────┐
│  Load garment   │─────▶│     Desize      │─────▶│      Dry        │
│ With pumice stone│      │                 │      │                 │
└─────────────────┘      └─────────────────┘      └────────┬────────┘
                                                            │
┌─────────────────┐      ┌─────────────────┐      ┌────────▼────────┐
│   Dry tumbler   │◀─────│ Cool with adding│◀─────│    Antichlor    │
│                 │      │     Water       │      │                 │
└────────┬────────┘      └─────────────────┘      └─────────────────┘
         │
┌────────▼────────┐      ┌─────────────────┐
│    Optical      │─────▶│    Softening    │
│   brightening   │      │                 │
└─────────────────┘      └─────────────────┘
```

Limitations of acid wash:

– Acid washed, indigo dyed denim has a tendency to yellow after wet processing.

– The major cause is residual manganese due to incomplete neutralization, washing or rinsing.

Remedy:

❖ Manganese is effectively removed during laundering with addition of ethelene-diamine-tetra-acetic acid as chelating agent.

❖ Acid washing jeans avoided some of problems of stone wash, but came with added dangers, expenses, and pollution.

4.2.5. Mechanical washes

4.2.5.1 Stone wash

❖ In the process of stone washing, freshly dyed jeans are loaded into large washing machines and tumbled with pumice stones to achieve a soft hand and desirable look.

❖ Variations in composition, hardness, size shape and porosity make these stones multifunctional. The process is quite expensive and requires high capital investment.

❖ Pumice stones give the additional effect of a faded or worn look as it abrades the surface of the jeans like sandpaper, removing some dye particles from the surfaces of the yarn.

Process cycle

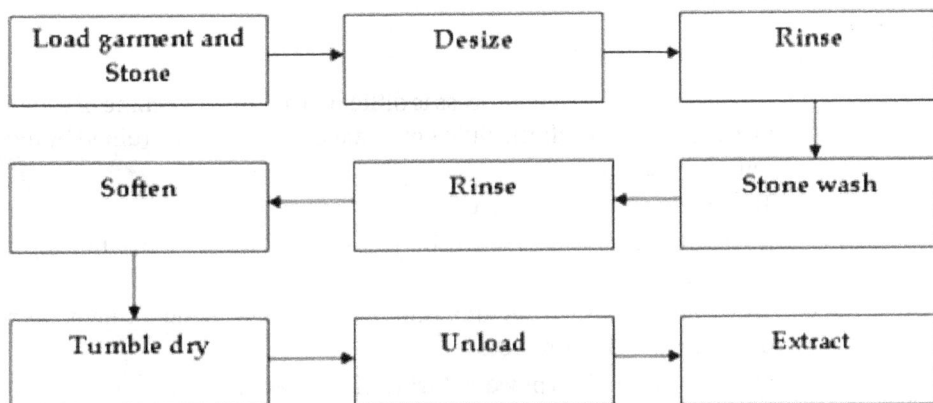

```
┌─────────────────┐      ┌─────────────────┐      ┌─────────────────┐
│ Load garment and│ ───> │     Desize      │ ───> │     Rinse       │
│     Stone       │      │                 │      │                 │
└─────────────────┘      └─────────────────┘      └─────────────────┘
                                                            │
                                                            ▼
┌─────────────────┐      ┌─────────────────┐      ┌─────────────────┐
│     Soften      │ <─── │     Rinse       │ <─── │   Stone wash    │
│                 │      │                 │      │                 │
└─────────────────┘      └─────────────────┘      └─────────────────┘
         │
         ▼
┌─────────────────┐      ┌─────────────────┐      ┌─────────────────┐
│   Tumble dry    │ ───> │     Unload      │ ───> │     Extract     │
│                 │      │                 │      │                 │
└─────────────────┘      └─────────────────┘      └─────────────────┘
```

Selection of stone

❖ Stone should be selected of the proper hardness, shape, and size for the particular end product. It should be noted that large, hard stones last longer and may be suited for heavy weight fabrics only.

❖ Smaller, softer stones would be used for light weight fabrics and more delicate items.

❖ Stone wt. /fabric wt. = 0.5 to 3 /1

❖ It depends on the degree of abrasion needed to achieve the desired result. Stones can be reused until they completely disintegrate or washed down the drain.

Problems caused by stones

❖ Damage to wash machineries and garment due to stone to machine and machine to stone abrasion

❖ Increase in labor to remove dust from finished garments.

❖ Water pollution during disposal of used liquor.

❖ Back staining and re deposition.

Back staining or Re-deposition

The dye removed from denim material after the treatment with cellulose or by a conventional washing process may cause "back staining or "redeposition. Re-coloration of blue threads and blue coloration of white threads, resulting in less contrast between blue and white threads.

Remedy of back staining

- ❖ Adding dispersion/suspension agent to wash cycle.
- ❖ Intermediate replacement of wash liquor.
- ❖ Using alkaline detergent like sodium per borate with optical brightener as after wash.

Limitations of stone washing:

- ❖ Quality of the abrasion process is difficult to control Outcome of a load of jeans is never uniform, little percentage always getting ruined by too much abrasion.
- ❖ The process is non-selective.
- ❖ Metal buttons and rivets on the jeans in the washing machines get abraded.
- ❖ This reduces quality of the products and life of equipment, and increases production costs.
- ❖ Stones may turn into powder during the process of making the garment grayish in color and rough too
- ❖ Provides rougher feel than enzyme wash
- ❖ Stone may lead the harm to the machine parts

4.2.6. Microsanding

There are 3 ways for this technique:

1. Sandblasting
2. Machine sanding
3. Hand sanding or hand brushing

Used in various ways:

- ❖ Flat surfaces (tables, ironing boards)
- ❖ On the dummy (inflatable dummies, sometimes standing, sometimes flat, sometimes 'seated')
- ❖ Various templates can be used to create a 3D effect.

4.2.7. Sand blasting

Sand blasting technique is based on blasting an abrasive material in granular, powdered or other form through a nozzle at very high speed and pressure onto specific areas of the garment surface to be treated to give the desired distressed/ abraded/ used look.

- ❖ It is purely mechanical process, not using any chemicals.
- ❖ It is a water free process therefore no drying required.
- ❖ Variety of distressed or abraded looks possible.
- ❖ Any number of designs could be created by special techniques.

4.2.8. Whiskering

❖ Also known as Cat's Whiskers
❖ Crease lines around the crotch.
❖ Industrially done with laser, sandblasting, machine sanding, hand sanding and abrasive rods.
❖ Also used for knee whiskers (whiskers on the sides of knees) and 'honeycombs' (crease marks on the back of the knee)

4.2.9. Other chemical washes:

❖ Rinse wash
❖ Cellulase wash
❖ Ozone fading
❖ Snow wash
❖ Salt water denim
❖ Flat finish
❖ Over dye
❖ Sun washing
❖ Super dark stone

Rinse wash

– Chemically bleaching jeans so that the color fades away

❖ Breaks down the fibers of jeans and creates white streaks or spots on denim
❖ Gives a unique rugged look, also called snow wash
❖ Earlier involved the use of pumice stone
❖ Presently process involves spraying chemical and removing it immediately
❖ Come in colors like blue, black, green, brown, grey *etc.*

Cellulase wash

❖ This is done to achieve a wash down appearance without the use of stones or with reduced quantities of stones.
❖ Cellulase enzymes are selective only to the cellulose and will not degrade starch.
❖ Under certain conditions, their ability to react with cellulose (cotton) will result in surface fiber removal (weight loss).
❖ This will give the garments a washed appearance and soft hand.

Factors influencing cellulase performance

❖ pH
❖ Temperature

- ❖ Time
- ❖ Dose
- ❖ Mechanical action

Ozone fading

- ❖ By using this technique, the garment can be bleached.
- ❖ Bleaching of denim garment is done in washing machine with ozone dissolved in water.
- ❖ Denim garments can also be bleached or faded by using ozone gas in closed chamber.
- ❖ In the presence of UV light, there is an interaction between the hydrocarbons, oxides of nitrogen and oxygen that causes release of ozone.
- ❖ Indigo dyestuff tends to fade or turn yellow due to ozone reaction.

The advantages associated with this process are:

- ❖ Color removal is possible without losing strength.
- ❖ This method is very simple and environmentally friendly because after laundering, ozonized water can easily be deozonized by UV radiation.

4.2.10. Flat finish

It is a special process done to impart fabric with an even wash down effect and very clean surface. Originally liquid ammonia was used, but now use mercerization plus calendering processes to achieve the flat surface.

Mercerization swells up the cotton fibers and allows the calendering to press flat the surface.

They consider this as an imitation process to the use of ammonia, which is toxic and not allowed in commercial use in most countries

Over dye

- ❖ Dyeing over the fabric or jeans to add another tone of color
- ❖ Most often used is a 'yellowy' overdye to create a 'dirty' look
- ❖ Also can be applied with spray gun or paintbrush for local coloring

Sun washing

- ❖ A very light shade by bleaching and stoning
- ❖ Looks as if the sun faded the fabric

Super dark stone

- ❖ Commercial term for an extra dark indigo color
- ❖ Results from a double-dyeing technique

Snow wash denim

Denim treated with a variation of acid wash that imparts bright white highlights.

Quick wash denim

❖ Aims at minimizing wash cycle time

❖ Results in more economical washes and solving many other washing problems faced by launderes during fashion wash cycles

❖ The yarns are ring dyed using indigo giving 25 to 30% less fixed dye to obtain a given shade

❖ During wash cycle,indigo dye can be removed quickly,giving washed look

Advantages of quick wash denim

1. Streaks develop in garments after washing process due to differences in dye concentration of denim fabrics are avoided using a modified alkali-ph controlled system giving uniformity of shade.

2. Amount of indigo dye required is less thus making it an economical process

3. Time required for washing is 20-30% less than that required for conventional denim.

4. Lesser enzymes and oxidising agent used

5. Environment friendly process

6. Back staining is minimised due to less concentration of of indigo dye in the wash liqour.

4.2.11. Other Mechanical washing

❖ Whiskering

❖ Shot gun denim

❖ Water jet fading

❖ Super stone wash

❖ Ice wash

❖ Thermo denim

❖ Laser technology finish

Water jet fading

❖ Hydrojet treatment is used for enhancing the surface finish, texture, durability of denim garment.

❖ Hydroject treatment involves exposing one or both surfaces of the garment through hydrojet nozzles.

❖ The degree of colour washout, clarity of patterns, and softness of the resulting fabric are related to the type of dye in the fabric and the amount and manner of fluid impact energy applied to the fabric.

❖ As this process is not involved with any chemical, it is pollution free.

Laser technology

❖ It is a computer controlled process for denim fading.

❖ This technique enables patterns to be created such as lines and/or dots, images, text or even pictures.

❖ It is water free fading of denim.

❖ Being an automatic system, chances of human error are slim.

❖ Also called spray painting in denims.

❖ This technique has relatively high cost.

Super stonewash

❖ Prolonged stonewashing, up to six hours or more.

Ice wash

❖ Ice washing in denim fabrics is done to remove more than half the dye during washing

Thermo-denim

❖ Also called double denim. A lightweight fabric (either plain, fancy or colored) is glued to the denim. The glue comes off after washing and the trousers look like they've been lined

Vintage

❖ Applies heavy stonewashing or a cellulose enzyme wash, with or without bleach

❖ Gives an old and worn look

4.2.12. Chemicals on denims

1. Bleach fast Indigo

❖ Value addition to denim

❖ Retains indigo on certain parts

❖ Kind of resist effect

❖ Chemical applied by brush, cured at 150C

❖ Ex. Indigofix AXN

2. Anti-depositing agent

❖ Prevents back staining of fabric by loose indigo during washing

❖ Improves contrast in denim

❖ Used in stone wash step

3. Dye stuffs with softener

❖   – To carry dyeing and softening in one step
❖   – Soft and supple hand
❖   – Saves time, money and energy as added to final rinse
❖   – Gives used and worn out effect

4. Anti creasing agent

❖   Provides fabric to fabric lubrication
❖   Prevents formation of crack marks and streaks
❖   Minimizes abrasion and gives strength

5. Wrinkle formation

❖   Creating smooth and permanent wrinkle
❖   Cross linking concept
❖   Ex. DMDHEU
❖   White pigment
❖   Can be applied by brush, spray or screen
❖   Then cured at 150°C
❖   Washed and treated with softener

6. White pigment

❖   Can be applied by brush, spray or screen
❖   Then cured at 150°C
❖   Washed and treated with softener

Denim is unique in its singular connection with one colour. The warp yarn is traditionally dyed with the blue pigment obtained from indigo dye. Until the introduction of synthetic dyes, at the end of the 19th century, indigo was the most significant natural dye known to mankind, linked with practical fabrics and work clothing. The durability of indigo as a color and it's darkness of tone made it a good choice, when frequent washing was not possible. The old mass market has segmented, fragmented, shattered into a multitude of mini, micro and niche markets. The last generation has a vast quantity of brands to choose from, a different perception of the cult value of owning small insider labels and a fanatical loyalty only to what's hot on a daily basis. Freed of all social and creative restrictions, denim is assuming any number of disguises and contexts to be worn in and has broken through almost any limitation on price. It can also be found in home collections, appearing in cushions, bed spreads and furniture-coverings.

4.3.   Fragrance finishing

Fragrance finishing of textile materials has been greatly expanded and used in recent years. Fragrance finishing can be done effectively using exhaust method than any other methods. If the fabric is treated with fragrance agents which exhibits higher durability of functionality is estimated. Fragrance finishing can be done by means of lavender aroma with non-ionic binder. This paper examines the effects of fragrance finished aloe-vera and cotton fabrics. Finally both the fragranced finished fabrics were made into wall hangings and the ambiance of the room was evaluated by comparing various factors. In this investigation, factors such as fabric performance, durability of the fragrance and laundering properties of the treated fabrics were investigated. The fragrance finished fabrics can be used in home textile applications such as wall hangings, table covers, carpets and sofa covers.

Gone are the days when quality product was the only criterion to eye a product by a consumer. Earlier were the times when sheer competitiveness in the domestic market was very confined. But, during some past years with the emergence of globalization, competitive atmosphere and quality consciousness, has reached a new mark. With the steady improvement in technology & application standards, a gradual rise was observed in consumer demands and to reach up to that mark, manufacturers have to add something to their products to get market value for their products. A product must be able to encompass something more with it & therefore this has taken today's market to a platform where it seems very difficult for a manufacturer to market his product until he satisfy the consumer with something new which not only rewards him for his novel concept but also lures him with considerable increase in profit . The role of the textile finisher has become increasingly demanding, and now requires a careful balance between the compatibility of different finishing products and treatments and the application processes used to provide textiles with desirable properties. Growing trends and escalating standards leave no stone unturned to boast the current scenario of textile industry. Performance with beauty describes the potential of textile finishing. Fragrance finishing of textiles is one such immaculate magnanimous entry into any textile culture. Fragrance finishing of textiles is the process where we enhance the value of the product by adding some incentives to it. The world market place is continuously changing and so is demand of people changing .Every person desires for some change .i.e. something new & unique. The successful effective implementation of change has to be done to in the market. We by the medium of this paper have made an earnest attempt to present you a detailed comprehensive analysis done by fragrance finishing and which has busted this industry with exuberant value added finish with the incorporation of different scents into fabrics, leading to the production of scented fabrics and the psychology of acceptance of synthetic scents in textile goods.

4.3.1. Technology for fragrance finishing (microencapsulation)

Microencapsulation is a natural phenomenon and the examples of ideal microcapsules are found in the nature i.e., spores, seeds, eggs and pollen etc only a few to mention. Due to numerous applications of microencapsulation and as a result there are a number of processes developed to encapsulate a galaxy of materials to suit the individual applicability. In the broadest sense, microencapsulation provides a means of packaging, separating and storing solid and liquid materials in a microscopic scale for a later release on your own desire under controlled conditions. The fragrance compound and the essential oil are volatile substances. The most difficult task in preparing the fragrance emitting textile is how to prolong its lifetime of Adour. Micro-encapsulation is an effective technique to solve this. Microcapsules are minute containers that are normally spherical if they enclose a liquid or gas, and roughly of the shape of the enclosed particle if they contain a solid. It can be considered as a special form of packaging, in that particulate matter can be individually coated for protection against environment and release the volatile substance from the enclosed capsule as required. This property has enabled microcapsules to serve many useful functions and find applications in different fields of technology. For example, the storage life of a volatile compound can be increased markedly by microencapsuling. The key to aromatic textile is how to make microcapsules of fragrance com-pounds and essential oils without omitting any ingredient in order to ensure its effects. In addition, using a low-temperature polymer binder to attach a perfumed microcapsule to the surface of the textile is also an important part of preparing an aromatic textile. At the same time, durability in laundering and a soft handle should be carefully considered

4.3.2. Microencapsulation Technology

1. Protection of the enclosed material and improved storage life.
2. Conversion of a liquid component to a dry solid system
3. Ensuring separation of incompatible components
4. Odor masking, dust control and pH control
5. Controlled diffusion of active components through the shell as for example in delayed drug release.

4.3.3. Applications of fragrance finishing:

Cosmeto-textiles

Microencapsulated skin moisturizers, vitamins and provitamins are applied in garments and known as cosmeto-textiles, designed for wear in contact with skin. These are claimed to promote a younger look, counteracting the effects of skin ageing, e.g. as a result of exposure to UV-radiation. There are also microencapsulated preparations for skin cooling.

Aromatherapy Textiles

The uses of aromatherapy textile are diverse. Interior textiles such as sheets, quilt-covers, curtains, carpets and bed-gowns are suitable for the attachment of lavender, camomile, citrus or cinnamon microcapsules, which are good for hypnogenesis and eliminating fatigue. Patients suffering high blood pressure feel sedation when they use a pillow made of fabric treated with lavender, basil, and lemon or fennel microcapsules. The tired office clerk wearing clothing with a scent of lemon rose, or jasmine oil may find his work efficiency improved. Meanwhile, it is convenient for dermatitis sufferers to be cured with the aid of underwear containing killing gem fabric. Perfumed toys make it easier for children to get closer to nature. Generally speaking, varied per-fume fabrics create good opportunities for customers to make the 'cocooning' environment they prefer to live in

Home Textiles

In other areas, household textiles such as curtains, sofas, cushions, sheets, as well as apparel items such as gloves, socks and ties may also be treated with microencapsulated fragrance and deodorizing finishes. The carpets can be finished with fragrances of different kinds and can be widely used in home textiles as well as automotive textiles.

Sport Wears

As the 'second skin' of the human body, all types of textile are excellent media for transferring fragrance compounds, and are essential to people in sport according to their preference for them. The type of the fragrance necessary for sportswear may be orange, lemon which will keep them energized on the ground for longer period

4.3.4. Process for Fragrance Finishing

Weaving

In the weaving process, the fabric is woven by plain weave with 60 ends per inch (EPI), 48 Picks per inch (PPI) and the yarn count used is 20s Ne (100 % cotton).

Desizing

Both the cotton fabrics are treated with de-sizing process for removing starch size. The fabric is padded with malt extract enzyme (3-5%) at 60°C by using 1:20 material to liquor ratio with pH 6-7. Finally the material is washed, squeezed and dried.

Scouring

After de-sizing the fabrics are treated with scouring process for remove the natural and added impurities present in fabric such as natural oils, wax, pectins, proteins, mineral matters, dirt *etc.* The fabric is treated with NaOH (2-3gm/l) and (2-3gm/l) non-ionic surfactant at 100°C for two hours by using 1: 20 material to liquor ratio with 12 pH. Finally the material is washed, squeezed and dried to get better absorbency.

Printing

The fabrics are printed with pigment colours by using direct style roller printing machine. And the fabrics were dried at 100°C, cured at 150°C for 4 to 5 minutes. Finally the fabrics are washed with 2% non-ionic surfactant and dried.

4.3.5. Methodology

Fragrance Finishing

Fragrance finishing is the process of imparting aroma in any textile substrate. This is done by exhaust method which means, fragrance agents is applied on both the cotton fabrics with the help of binder. Lavender fragrance was taken as a flavor for this process.

Preparation of Recipe

The lavender fragrance agents with binder ST were formed by mixture solution containing alcohol and distilled water with ratio (1:3). The solution was emulsified with a high-speed mixer at a speed of about 10,000 rpm for 5 minutes. The emulsified system was transferred into a flask. The alcoholic fragrance solution was added into the emulsified solutions over 30 minutes, and stirred at a temperature of 40°C for 2 hours.

Finishing Process

Fragrance finishing was given to the fabric by exhaustion method with 5-7% binder ST which is used as cross-linking agent. The fabrics were kept immersed in the solution containing lavender fragrance, (ML ratio – 1: 10) for 20-30 minutes at 40°C in water bath. After finishing, the fabrics were removed, squeezed and dried at 100°C in the oven for 5 minutes and then cured at 120 °C for 2 minutes

Fragrance finish is the process by which textile materials are treated with the pleasant odors which yields better beneficial effects. The pleasant smells can be created by the essential oils have pharmacological effects like antibacterial, antifungal, antiviral, *etc.* and mood elevating effects. The fragrance of lavender proves good way to meet important psychological and emotional needs, as well as those of a purely physical and sensorial nature. Thus by comparing the laundering durability results, it justifies that fragrance finished aloe-vera fabric has better laundering durability. Comparing the sensorial effect of fragrance intensity, it justifies that fragrance finished aloe-vera fabric has better sensorial effect of fragrance intensity. Then based on the washing fastness results, it justifies that fragrance finished aloe-vera fabric has better adjacent fabrics staining rating than cotton fabric. Comparing the light fastness rating, it justifies that fragrance finished cotton fabric has slightly better light fastness rating than aloe-vera fabric. Based on the wick-ability results, it justifies that wick-ability were good for both fabrics. Finally based on the overall performance it is concluded that the fragrance finished aloe-vera fabric is better than cotton fabric for wall hanging (curtain) and in all home textile applications.

4.4. UV protection finishes

The sunlight is essential for life and is important for human health, as the body needs it to form Vitamin-D, enhance circulation of blood, invigorate the metabolism and improve resistance to various pathogens. At the same time, ultraviolet rays contained in sunlight pose a major stress and risk potential for the skin. Due to the change in the way people are spending their leisure time, dermatologists are recording a significant increase in the number of cancer cases worldwide. Dermatologists and anti-cancer organisations therefore warn against excessive exposure of the sun and call for prevention by means of suitable clothing and sun protective textiles. This is particularly important for children and for the people who spend a lot of time outdoors in their line of work, such as construction workers, road workers or gardeners to use textile for sun protection.

The risks posed by ultraviolet radiation have become more dangerous in recent years as the whole world is suffering from all kinds of pollution. Clothing has the ability to protect the skin from incident solar radiation because the fabric from which it is made can reflect, absorb and scatter solar wavelengths. Each fabric must be tested to determine its ability to protect from solar radiation, as this cannot be known from visual observation nor calculated from descriptions of the fabric's composition and structure. To determine this so called Ultraviolet Protection Factor (UPF), special test standards and methods are required as offered by different associations. Care labelling similar to fabric and garment care labels has been developed for UV protection, and standard procedures have been established for the measurement, calculation, labelling methods and comparison of label values.

4.4.1. Ultraviolet radiation

Ultraviolet radiation is the one form of radiant energy coming out from the sun. The sun emits a range of energy known as the electromagnetic spectrum. The various forms of energy, or radiation, are classified according to wavelength. The shorter the wave-length, the more energetic the radiation. Sunlight that reaches the earth is composed of 66% of infrared light, 32% visible light, and 2% ultraviolet light (UVL). Ultraviolet, which is invisible, is so named because it occurs next to violet in the visible light spectrum. The three categories of UV radiation are:

1. UV-A (320-400 nm)

UV-A rays are the least powerful of the UV rays, but they are present all year and can penetrate windows and clouds. They penetrate more deeply into the skin and contribute to premature aging of the skin and skin cancers.

2. UV-B (280-320 nm)

UV-B rays are the most powerful and potentially harmful form of radiation. It is the most common cause of sunburn, aging, wrinkling and skin cancer. UVB is particularly strong at the equator, at high elevations or during the summer.

3. UV-C (200-280 nm)

UV-C rays are the shortest and most powerful of the UV rays. UV-C is the most likely to cause cancer if it reaches skin. Fortunately, most of it is absorbed by the ozone layer in our atmosphere. Ozone depletion has created a growing ozone "Hole" near the South Pole due to this, intensity and frequency of sun-related cancers will increase.

4.4.2. Factors that affect solar ultraviolet radiation

Geographical position: If a part of earth is closer to the equator, the UV radiation will be more in comparison of other part. Australia has higher level of solar UVR in comparison with Europe and North America mainly due to its geographical position.

Sun Height

When the sun remains high in the sky, the UV radiation found shorter distance to travel through so less UVR is absorbed and more passes to earth.

Ozone

Ozone is a form of oxygen that occurs naturally in the upper atmosphere and has the ability to absorb UV radiation. Ozone levels rise and fall naturally from day to day and seasonally. Atmospheric absorption prevents most of UV radiation to reach to the ground level.

Elevation

There is more UV radiation at higher elevations than at lower elevations because more UV radiation is scattered and the smaller the amount reaches to the surface.

Clouds

Clouds are made up of millions of water droplets. It can transmit, reflect and scatter UV radiation. The amount of each is dependent upon the thickness of the cloud and its morphology. Generally, the larger and thicker the cloud is, the lesser amount of UV radiation is transmitted.

Dust/Haze

These two conditions act on UV radiation the same way as they both scatter UV radiation. There is less UV radiation on hazy or dusty days reaching the surface than on a clear day.

Air Pollution/Smog

Emissions from traffic and manufacturing plants form smog by chemical reactions with the help of UV radiation & heat. As a result, the amount of UV radiation reaching the surface is smaller under these conditions, but this condition is not favorable for our environment.

4.4.3. Requirement and selection of a ideal UV absorber

1. An effective UV absorber has to be absorb through out the spectrum to remain stable against UVR and then to dissipate the absorbed energy to avoid degradation of fabric or loss of color value.

2. Highest absorbency in the ultraviolet region {290-340nm} and no absorbency in the visible region.

3. Should be heat stable and compatible with other additives in the finish formulation

4. Should be non toxic and non- skin irritant.

4.4.4. Types of UV absorbers

Organic UV absorbers are derivatives of o- hydroxyl benzophenones, o – hydroxyphenyltriazes, o – hydroxy phenyl hydrazines. The ortho hydroxyl group in the molecule helps in absorption and to make the compound soluble in alkaline solution. Organic compounds like benzotriazole, hydro benzophenone and phenyltriazine can be used by normal padding or coating applications. Ortho hydroxyphenyl and diphenyltriazine derivatives have excellent sublimation fastness and self dispersing formulation. It can be applied by pad thermosol process and also in print pastes. The presence of in organic pigments in the fibers helps in better diffusion of light from the substrate, thus providing better protection. Titanium dioxide and other ceramic materials have an absorption capacity in the UV region of 280-400nm and reflects visible and IR rays.

4.4.5. Hazards of UVR to human

Human skin is the body's largest organ and acts simultaneously as a barrier against and an interface with the environment. Three main layers are: epidermis (0.1-1.5 mm), corium (4-8 mm) and subcutis. Corium and subcutis are collectively called as dermis. Visible and IR radiations can easily penetrate through the skin layers. However, UV light differs in that it is absorbed in the epidermis and corium. UV-B radiations penetrate less deeply into the epidermis than UV-A radiation (Figure 1). Increased penetration of solar UV-B radiation is likely to have profound impact on human health with potential risks of eye diseases, skin cancer and infectious diseases. UV radiation is known to damage the cornea and lens of the eye. UV-B radiation can adversely affect the immune system causing a number of infectious diseases. Excessive UV radiation leads to cell damage and causes inflammation of human skin, the obvious consequences of which are erythema or sunburn. Relation between different UV radiations and response of human skin towards those radiations. UV-B is the strongest in comparison with the UV-A & UV-C.

4.4.6. Solar UV Index

The UV index is designed to provide the public with a numerical indication of the maximum potential solar UVR level during the day; the higher the number, the higher the solar UVR hazard. The global solar UV Index is a measure of the highest level of UVR every day, and the UV Index is calculated using various input parameters such as the ozone level, potential cloud cover, water vapour, aerosols and the elevation of cities. The UVR is usually highest around midday but the temperature is often highest later in the afternoon. UVR index values are grouped into five exposure categories, from low to extreme with different colour codes. UV-Index is a measure of the maximum daily level of ultraviolet radiation (UVR). When the UV level reaches 3 or higher a combination of five sun protection measures (sun protective clothing, hat, sunglasses, sunscreen and shade) may be required for personal protection. Adequate amount of UV radiation is present in India for at least 10 months a year. UV Index for India is given by Global Ozone Measurement Experiment, which was taken throughout the year. UV index ranges from moderate to extreme throughout all parts of India. Maximum during the months from March to September, the reason may be the intensity of the sun become higher due to the position of earth and sun during that time period. Difference is visible among the difference regions of India because of Elevation and Geographical position.

4.4.7. Ultraviolet protection factor

The protection extended by the textile materials are denoted by Ultraviolet Protection Factor (UPF). UPF measures the amount of UV radiation that penetrates a fabric and reaches the skin. UPF measures both UV-A & UV-B radiation blocked. UPF rating does not refer to the design of the garment; it is just its material. A fabric with a UPF 15 allows only 1/15th (6.66%) of the UV-radiation to penetrate the skin as compared to uncovered skin.

4.4.8. Solar Protection Factor

SPF stands for sun/solar protection factor and is the rating we are familiar with for sunscreens and other sun-protective products. SPF is a measurement of UV-B radiation only . The solar protection factor (SPF) is defined as the ratio of the length of time of solar radiation exposure required for the skin to show redness (erythema) with and without protection. Mathematically, SPF can be calculated as follows:

SPF = MED Protected Skin/MED Unprotected Skin

Where, MED represents minimal erithemal dose

MED is defined as the minimum quantity of radiant energy required to produce first detectable reddening of the skin, 22 ± 2 hours after exposure.

4.4.9. Protective measures

❖ Simple precautions will prevent both short-term and long-term damage of UV radiation exposure, while still making the time spent outdoors enjoyable. Sun protection is important in all settings, in particular at all outdoor recreation sites such as beaches and sports centers. The basic sun protection can be done by:

❖ Seeking shade & limiting exposure during midday hours.

❖ Wearing a broad brimmed hat to protect the eyes, face and neck.

❖ Protecting the eyes with sunglasses.

❖ Using and reapplying sunscreen of SPF 15+.

❖ Protecting babies and young children using appropriate protective clothing having UPF value of at least 15.

❖ Different sources provide different UV-radiation, among all the source UV protection provided by UV protective clothing is highest.

4.4.10. Textile materials & UV protection

Mechanism of UV protection

When radiations strikes a fibre surface, it can be reflected, absorbed, transmitted through the fibre & pass between fibres. The relative amounts of radiation reflected, absorbed or transmitted depend on many factors, including the fibre type, the fibre surface smoothness, the fabric cover factor and the presence or absence of fibre delustrants, dyes and UV absorbers. The UVR transmitted through textile fabrics consists of the unchanged waves that pass through the interstices of the fabrics as well as scattered waves that have interacted with the fabrics. Another part is absorbed when it penetrates the sample, and is converted into a different energy form. The portion of radiation that travels through the fabric and reaches the skin is appropriately referred to as the 'Transmission component'.

4.4.11. Degradation of textile material by UV radiation

UV radiation is one of the major causes of degradation of textile materials, which is due to excitations in some parts of the polymer molecule and a gradual loss of integrity, and depends on the nature of the fibres. Because of the very large surface volume ratio, textile materials are susceptible to influences from light and other environmental factors. The penetration of UVR in nylon causes photo oxidation and results in decrease in elasticity, tensile strength and a slight increase in the degree of crystallinity. In the absence of UV filters, the loss in tensile strength appears to be higher in the case of nylon (100% loss), followed by polyester (44%), cotton (34%) & wool (23%) after 30 days of exposure.

4.4.12. Important parameters for UV protective clothing

Important parameters on which UV protection by textile material depends are described as follows:

4.4.12.1 Nature of fibres

In textiles, UPF is strongly dependent on the chemical structure of the fibres. The nature of the fibres influences the UPFs as they vary in UV transparency. Natural fibres like cotton, silk, and wool have lower degree UVR absorption than synthetic fibres such as PET because PET have aromatic group in its molecular structure. Cotton fabric in a grey state provides a higher UPF because the natural pigments, pectin, and waxes act as UV absorbers, while bleached fibres have high UV transparency. Raw natural fibres like linen and hemp possess a UPF of 20 and 10-15 respectively, and are not perfect UV protectors even with lignin content. However, the strong absorption of jute is due to the presence of lignin, which acts as a natural absorber. Protein fibres also have mixed effects in allowing UV radiation. Wool absorbs strongly in the region of 280-400 nm and even beyond 400 nm & have UPF value of 45-50+. Exposure to sunlight damages the quality of silk's colour, strength and resiliency in both dry and wet conditions. Mulberry silk is deteriorated to a greater extent than muga silk. Bleached silk and bleached polyacrylonitrile show very low UPFs of 9.4 and 3.9 respectively. Polyester fibres absorb more in the UV-A & UV-B regions than aliphatic polyamide fibres because of the presence of aromatic group in its molecular structure.

4.4.12.2 Fabric construction factors

Fabric construction factors are the ost important determinant of UV-Radiation. It includes weave, weave density, cover factor, porosity, weight and thickness. All the factors are interrelated and influence each other.

4.4.12.3 Weave and weave density

Closer the fabric's weave, the higher the UV radiation protection because the fibres of tightly woven fabrics are closer together, less UV radiation is able to pass through to the skin. Twill weave is much denser than satin/sateen weave due to its compactness hence; less UVR is transmitted through twill weave than satin/sateen weave. For the woven fabrics of same weight, the plain weave designs give the highest protection. Tightly woven, light-weight fabrics such as linen, cotton or hemp will also provide sufficient UV protection. Knitted or woven fabrics alter protection due to interlacing – the open spaces where yarns cross. These tiny gaps let the fabric breathe, increasing comfort, and unfortunately increasing UV transmission as well. Stretched areas in a garment pull at the interlacing, permitting UV to penetrate. Woven fabrics are more UV protective than knitted fabrics.

4.4.12.4 Cover factor

Cover factor is defined as the percentage area occupied by warp and weft yarns in a given fabric area. Cover factor should be the primary determinant of protectiveness against UVR transmission. To understand the relationship between UVR transmission and fabric structure, an ideal fabric is proposed. This ideal fabric is one in which the yarns are completely opaque to UV and the holes or spaces between the yarns are very small. UVR transmission through ideal fabric is related to the cover factor of the ideal fabric with opaque yarns as follows:

% UVR transmission = 100-cover factor

The UPF of the ideal fabric is related to % transmission as:

UPF = 100/% transmission

Hence,

UPF = 100/ (100-Cover factor)

UPF values of 200, 40, 20 and 10 can be achieved with the percentage cover factors of 99.5, 97.5, 95 and 90 respectively. Woven fabrics usually have a higher cover factor than knits due to the type of construction. To achieve a minimum UPF rating of 15, the cover factor of the textile must be greater than 93%, and a very small increase in Cover factor leads to substantial improvements in the UPF of the textiles above 95% cover factor. In the case of terry cloth, a high variability in UPF exists due to irregularities in the fabric construction. Woven fabrics usually have a higher cover factor than knits due to the type of construction. Knitted structure made from a blend of synthetic fibres with Lycra offers the best protection against solar radiation. Stretching or tension reduces the UPF rating of the fabric during wear, as the effective cover factor is reduced. This is common in knitted or elasticised fabrics.

4.4.12.5 Porosity, Weight and Thickness

The UPF increases with fabric density and thickness for similar construction, and is dependent on porosity (UPF = 100 / porosity). A high correlation exists between the UPF and the fabric porosity but is also influenced by the type of fibres. The relative order of importance for the UV protection is given by % cover > fibre type > fabric thickness. A UPF with fabric weight and thickness shows better correlation than cloth cover. Therefore fabrics with the maximum number of yarns in warp and weft give high UPFs. Fabric weight and thickness are minor factor. Higher weight and thicker fabrics have better ultraviolet protection.

4.4.12.6 Dyeing and finishing

UV protection ability of textile materials are influenced by the type of dye or pigment, the absorptive groups present in the dyestuff, depth after dyeing, the uniformity and additives present in the finishes. A protective effect can be obtained by dyeing, printing or finishing, which is better than using heavyweight fabrics which are not suitable for summer conditions.

4.4.12.7 Colour and Dyes

Generally Dark colours (black, navy, dark red) of the same fabric type provide better UV protection than the light pastel colours (white, sky blue, light green) for identical weave due to increased UV absorption. For instance, the UPF of a green colour T-shirt is 10 versus 7 for white. However, particular dyes can vary considerably in the degree of UV protectiveness because of individual transmission and absorption characteristics. Some direct, reactive and vat dyes are capable of giving a UPF of 50+. Some of the direct dyes substantially increase the UPF of bleached cloth, which depends on the relative transmittance of the dyes in the UV-B region. In many cases, a UPF calculated using a direct dye solution appears to be higher than that of the fabric after dyeing, mainly because the actual concentrations are mostly less than the theoretical concentration. Dyes extracted from various natural resources also show the UPF within the range of 15 – 45 depending on the mordant used.

4.4.13. UV Stabilisers

Several types of UV stabilisers are available, the most common being benzophenones and phenyl benzotriazoles. These molecules are able to absorb the damaging UV rays of sunlight.

4.4.14. Classification of UV stabilisers

Ultraviolet stabilisers can be classified into three different categories depending on their mode of action.

4.4.14.1 UV Absorbers

The amount of UV radiations absorbed by a polymer upon natural weathering can be reduced substantially by using additives, which compete with the photosensitive chromophores of the polymer substrate for the absorption of the incident photons. The UV absorbers provide long-term stabilisation against the UV radiations without getting destroyed. UV absorbers are organic or inorganic colourless compounds with very strong absorption in the UV range of 290 – 360nm. UV absorbers incorporated in to the fibres convert electronic excitation energy in to thermal energy. They function as radical scavengers and oxygen scavengers. The high-energy short wave UVR excites the UV absorber to a high energy absorbed may then be dissipated as longer wave radiation. Alternatively, isomerisation can occur and the UV absorber may then fragment in to non- absorbing isomers. Organic UV absorbers are derivatives of o-hydroxyl benzophenones, o-hydroxyphenyltriazes, and o-hydroxy phenyl hydrazines. Titanium dioxide and other ceramic materials have an absorption capacity in the UV region of 280- 400nm and reflects visible and IR rays. UV absorbers for synthetic fibres are Phenyl salicylates, benzophenones, benzotriazoles, cyanoacrylates, phenyltriazines. UV absorbers for natural fibres are benzotriazole derivatives, Oxalic acid dianilide derivatives. UV absorbers incorporated in dyeing decreases the dye uptake, except in post treatment application. They are compatible with dyes and are applied by normal padding, exhaust, pad thermosol, pad dry cure methods. UV absorbers are applied between 30-40g/l depending on the type of fibre and its construction. The main limitations of UV absorbers are that they cannot be applied in a single bath along with other finishing agents; anything in excess will have a detrimental effect on the fabric. With the advent of nano science and technology, a new area has developed in the area of textile finishing called Nano finishing. Coating the surface of textiles and clothing with nano particles is an approach to the production of highly active surfaces to have UV blocking properties. Metal oxides like ZnO as UV blocker are more stable as compared to organic UV blocking agents. Zinc oxide (ZnO) nano particles embedded in polymer matrices like soluble starch will enhance the UV blocking property due to their increase surface area and intense absorption in the UV region.

4.4.14.2 Quenchers

The excited chromophores (C*) responsible for photo oxidation can transfer their energy to an adequate accepter or quencher (Q), before chemical bonds are broken and radical initiated reaction proceed. For effective stabilisation, it is important that further deactivation of the excited quencher to the ground state molecule occur without the production of any reactive species. The commonly used light stabilisers of this kind are organic complexes of transition metals like Ni, Fe, Cr *etc.* The inherent colour of these metal complexes is a distinct problem, which limits their use as stabilisers for white and clear polymer materials.

4.4.14.3 Hindered Amine Light Stabilisers (HALs)

Derivatives of 2, 2, 6, 6-tetramethylpiperidine are called HALs. HALs protects polymer chemically not physically and their effectiveness depends on the optimum dispersal in the binding agents. HALs are extremely efficient at preventing light induced degradation of most polymers. They do not absorb UV radiation, but instead act to inhibit degradation of the polymer. The basic principle followed here is:

- ❖ They form nitroxyl radicals in the reaction with hydroperoxides.
- ❖ These nitroxyl radicals react with free radicals in the polymer backbone to form amine ethers.
- ❖ The amine ethers terminate peroxy radicals to cause reversion to nitroxyl radicals.

4.4.15. Wearing conditions

The ability of textile fibres to provide UV protection varies depending upon the structure and other additives present in the fibres. Besides, the construction parameters and wear conditions of the textile materials, moisture and additives incorporated in processing also affect the UPF of the textile materials.

4.4.16. Wetness and moisture

When textiles becomes wet by air hydration, perspiration, or water, UV transmission through the fabric can significantly change, with a marked reduction of UPF observed for textiles made from cotton and cotton blends. In the case of moisture, the influence largely depends on the type and hygroscopicity of fibres, as well as conditioning time, which result in swelling phenomena. The Relative humidity and moisture content affect the UPF of the fabric in two ways, namely the swelling of fibres due to moisture absorption, which reduces the interstices, and consequently the UV transmittance. On the other hand, the presence of water reduces scattering effects, as the refractive index of water is closer to that of the textile polymer, and hence there is a greater UV transmission in comparison to a lower UPF. In Florida, it is a common practice for parents to put a white T-shirt on their children to protect them from the sun while swimming. But when that T-shirt gets wet, it provides a UPF of only 3. A typical cotton fabric could transmit 15-20% UVR, rising to more than 50% if the garment is wet. For adequate protection, the UVR transmission should be lower than 6% and 2.5% for extremely good protection. Dependence of humidity is more pronounced in silk and viscose, of which viscose has a higher water absorption and swelling capacity, while silk has poor swelling properties. Even though silk has poor swelling properties, it's very fine nature and a greater number of fibres in the cross-section of yarn results in higher swelling due to capillary absorption, and in turn less UV transmittance. In general, hygroscopic fibres and their UPF show better correlation.

4.4.17. Stretch

Stretching or tension reduces the UPF rating of the fabric during wear. It is common in knitted or elasticised fabrics.

4.4.18. Laundering

Fabrics undergo a combination of relaxation and consolidation shrinkage when washed hence UPF increase after first laundering and remain constant after subsequent washing. Laundering garment with detergent containing optical fluorescent brighteners improve UV protection. A laundry additive Sun Guard contains the sunscreen Tinosorb ® FD, when added to detergent it increases the UPF of clothing & this protection lasts through 20 washing.

4.4.19. Apparel Design

Clothing provides an even, non-sticky form of protection that does not have to be reapplied. Good quality sun protection clothing typically covers a maximum amount of skin. Yet is to be designed to be cool and comfortable to wear. Collared shirts and at least three quarter length trousers and three-quarter length sleeve tops cover skin well. Shirt with long sleeves and a large collar offers much better protection. Loose-fitting clothes give better protection than closefitting clothes and may be more comfortable to wear on hot days. Techniques for quantitative measurement of UVR transmission Various techniques, both qualitative and quantitative, have been used to measure the UVR blocking capability of fabrics and to calculate a UVR protection factor. Quantitative testing of fabrics has been carried out using techniques such as, In vivo testing and In vitro testing which constitutes radiometric measurements and Spectrophotometric measurements. The instrument for measuring fabric transmission includes broadband radiometers, spectroradiometers, or spectophotometers, and Xenon lamps. Filters are placed next to the test specimen to prevent the effects of fluorescence reaching the integrating sphere. The spectral response of the detector is also important in determining system performance, and it must be capable of detecting UVR accurately and linearly over a very large range of intensities and discriminating the signal from the detector dark current. The preparation of the fabric prior to the UV transmission test includes the exposure of specimen to laundering, simulated sunlight and chlorinated pool water, and to present in a state that simulate the conditions at the end of two years of normal seasonal use, so that the UV protection level finally stated on the label estimates the maximum transmittance of the garment fabric during a two-year life cycle.

4.4.20. UV protection care labeling

Initiatives for developing standards related to UV protection started in the 1990s, and standards related to the preparation of fabrics, testing and guidance for UV protection labelling have been formulated by different agencies. Care labelling similar to fabric and garment care labels has been developed for UV protection, and standard procedures have been established for the measurement, calculation, labelling methods and comparison of label values of textile products. Since 1981, the Skin

Cancer Foundation, an international body, has offered a Seal of Recommendation for the photo-protective products, which includes sunscreens, sunglasses, window films and laundry detergent additives, in accordance with AATCC TM 183 or AS/NZS 4399; The products recommended are reviewed annually. The Australian/New Zealand Standard for sun protective clothing (AS/NZS 4399) also describes methods and labelling requirements for UPF rated clothing.

UV labelling is an additional requirement besides other labelling requirements of garment including Permanent Care Labels and Fibre Content labels. Table 8. shows the various grades and the related protection factors for the textile materials. The UPF value to be placed on the label is that of the sample, reduced by its standard error of UPF values, and then rounded down to the nearest multiple of 5 but not greater than 50. A UPF of 20 means that 1/20th, ie, 5%, of the biologically effective UV radiation striking the surface of the fabric actually passes through it.

The best technique for reducing UV exposure is to avoid sun exposure, but this is an unacceptable solution to all. Recreational exposure accounts for most of the significant UVR exposures of the population, and occupational exposure is also significant. UVR exposure can be reduced by creating awareness among people about the hazardous effect of UV radiations & by implementing by behavioural change such as avoiding sunlight at its maximum, using protection such as hats, sunscreens, sun glasses, and clothing. In India UV Index is less than the other places of world such as Australia and Switzerland, because of its geographical position but the percentage of farmers and outdoor workers are higher than those places. So, there is need to design special clothing for Indian condition for effective UV protection. Farmers and outdoor workers are less aware about the hazardous effect of UV radiation, there is need to aware them.

Methodology

Identification of UV Absorber
↓
Padding technique
↓
Extraction
↓
Tests
↓
UPF test – (untreated, treated fabric)

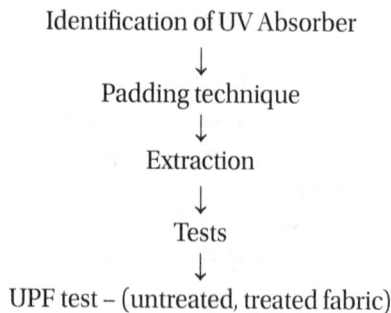

4.4.21. Selection of Natural UV Absorber

Green tea

Botanical name : Theaceae

Family : Sinensis

Parts used : Leaves

Source

It is a large shrub with white flowers and is indigenous to Asia and China, but commercially grown in Africa, Srilanka, Malaysia and Indonesia.

Composition

The tannins interact with proteins and are astringent and also have antioxidant activity. One of the polyphenols in green tea – epigallocatechin galate (EGCG) is thought to be 200 times more powerful than Vitamin E for neutralizing free radicals. It contains caffeine as well as triterpene saponins, carotenoids and non-protein amino acids (theanine, 2-amino-6-ethylamidoadipinic acid).

Epigallocatechin galate (EGCG) Properties

❖ EGCG is a type of catechin
❖ Found in tea and other plants
❖ It is a powerful antioxidant
❖ It inhibits the growth of cancer cells
❖ It has been effective in lowering LDL cholesterol levels
❖ It also inhibits the abnormal formation of blood clots.

Chemical formula: $C_{22}H_{18}O_{11}$

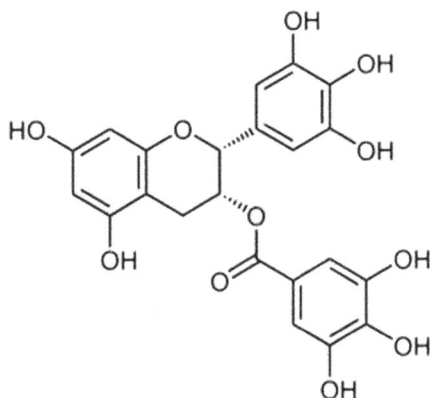

Chemical structure of Epigallocatechin galate

Beetroot

Botanical name: *Beta vulgaris*

Family : Sinensis

Parts used : Vegetable

Source and description

The red beet, commonly known as garden beet, is a juicy root vegetable. It is distinguished by its individual flavor. It is more colorful than other root vegetables.

Beets have several varieties, which are grouped according to their shapes. They are flat, short top shaped, deep oblate to round, globular to oval, and half long. The two varieties, most commonly grown in India are crimson globe and Detroit dark red, both belonging to the globular to oval group.

Composition

It has contain betacyanin and various other types of nutrition such as vitamins, minerals, iron, zinc, calcium, sodium, carbohydrates, proteins, folacin, niacin and more.

Betacyanin properties

❖ Betacyanin is the pigment that gives beets their rich purple-crimson colour.

❖ It is a powerful anti-oxidant

❖ It is used as a natural food dye

❖ It is a powerful cancer-fighting agent

❖ It can increase the oxygen-carrying ability of the blood by up to 400 percent.

❖ They help in normalizing blood pressure.

Chemical formula: $C_{15}H_{24}O$

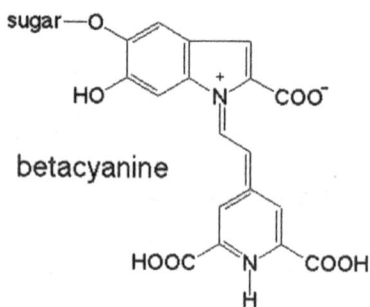

betacyanine

Chamomile

Botanical name : *Anthemis nobilis*

Family : N.O. Compositae

Parts used : Flower

Source and description

The plant produces a round, furrowed, and branched stem which grows one to two feet in height. The leaves are pale green, incised, and sessile, with thread-shaped leaflets. The flower heads consists of yellow disk flowers and white petal-shaped ray flowers that are bent downward to make the disk flowers more prominent part is the flower.

Composition

It has contained Flavonoids, coumarins, essential, oils and polysaccharides are characteristic compound in the chemical composition of chamomile.

Flavonoid properties

1. Flavonoids are the most important plant pigments for flower coloration.
2. It produces yellow or red with blue pigmentation in petals designed to attract pollination animals.
3. Also helps in following
   - ❖ Anti-oxidant activities
   - ❖ Anti-allergic activities
   - ❖ Anti-inflammatory activities
   - ❖ Anti-microbial activities
   - ❖ Anti-cancer activities

Chemical formula: $C_{15}H_{10}O_7$

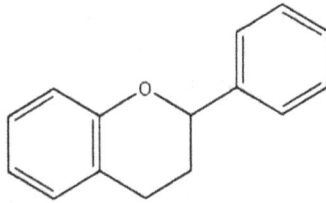

Chemical structure of Flavonoid

4.4.21.1 Extraction Method

- ❖ About 100 grams of each one of green tea leaves, beetroot, and chamomile flowers are taken separately.
- ❖ 250ml of water is taken (approximately twice the amount of material)
- ❖ Boiled for 15 minutes till it reaches the boiling temperature.
- ❖ It's then filtered and the extract is taken out separately.

4.4.21.2 Padding Technique

Padding is a method adopted to apply the herbal extracts onto the fabric and give them the required properties. Padding mangle is used for this process.

4.4.21.3 Testing Instrument

- ❖ UV transmittance analyzer
- ❖ UV-visible spectrophotometer (or) spectroradiometer
- ❖ These have use of flash xenon lamp, it has provided to be the best alternative for reproduction of natural sunlight.

4.4.21.4 Testing Standard

1. This standard test method AATCC 183:2004 is used to determine the ultraviolet radiation blocked or transmitted by textile fabrics intended to be used for UV protection.
2. This method provides procedures for measuring this fabric property with specimen in either the dry or wet states.

4.5 Phase Change finishes

Phase change materials (PCMs) materials have high heats of fusion so they can absorb a lot of energy before melting or solidifying. A PCM temperature remains constant during the phase change, which is useful for keeping the subject at a uniform temperature. It is one of the application of technical textile. PCM have been studied for use in direct thermal energy storage, solar energy applications and more recently, in response to growing international concern to climate change, building temperature regulation .PCM can undergo solid-solid, liquid-gas and solid-liquid transformations. Solid-solid PCMs generally have high transition temperatures which are beyond the scope of practical use. Liquid-gas PCMs are not considered usable for most applications due to the large volume change that occurs at phase change. Solid-liquid PCMs have seen the most use in research and applications as they have high latent heat capacities and good thermal conductivity, making them practical for use. There are however several difficulties that can arise when using certain solid-liquid PCMs such as, subcooling, phase segregation and corrosiveness.

Energy and environment are the two major issues facing human beings nowadays. Industrial developments and population boom in the past few centuries have resulted in an enormous increase in energy demand with an annual increasing rate at about 2.3%. The increasing demand for energy-saving and environment-friendly technology is driving the growth of the global phase change material (PCM) market. The global PCM market is expected to grow from $300.8 million in 2009 to $1,488.1 million in 2015, at an estimated CAGR of 31.7% from 2010 to 2015. The paraffin-based PCM market commands the largest share of the overall PCM market in terms of value, while salt hydrate-based PCMs lead the market in terms of volume. Building and construction currently forms the largest application market due to the globally increasing demand for cooling buildings, which in turn has arisen due to the shift from heavy thermal mass design to lightweight architecture. While this application contributed 22% to the global PCM market revenues in 2009, textile applications are expected to have the highest CAGR of 38.5% from 2010 to 2015.On this occasion, scientists had begun to research in renewable energy technologies in order to turn the tide of climate change and achieve a sustainable development for human beings. Phase Change Materials (PCMs) provides a high heat storage density and has the capability of storing a large amount of heat during the phase change process with a small variation of PCM volume and temperature.

4.5.1. PCM Materials and their characteristics

Different kinds of materials were used as PCM. In principal materials should fulfill different criteria in order to be suitable to serve as a PCM.

1. Suitable melting temperature
2. High melting enthalpy per volume unit [kJ/m^3]
3. High specific heat [kJ/(kg.K)]
4. Low volume change due to the phase change
5. High thermal conductivity
6. Cycling stability
7. Not flammable, not poisonous
8. Not corrosive

As one of the goals of latent energy storage is to achieve a high storage density in a relatively small volume, PCMs should have a high melting enthalpy [kJ/kg] and a high density [kg/m^3], i.e. a high volumetric melting enthalpy [kJ/m^3].

4.5.2. Classification of PCM

Based on phase change state, PCMs fall into three groups: solid- solid PCMs, solid–liquid PCMs and liquid–gas PCMs. Among them the solid–liquid PCMs are most suitable for thermal energy storage. The solid–liquid PCMs comprise organic PCMs, inorganic PCMs and eutectics.

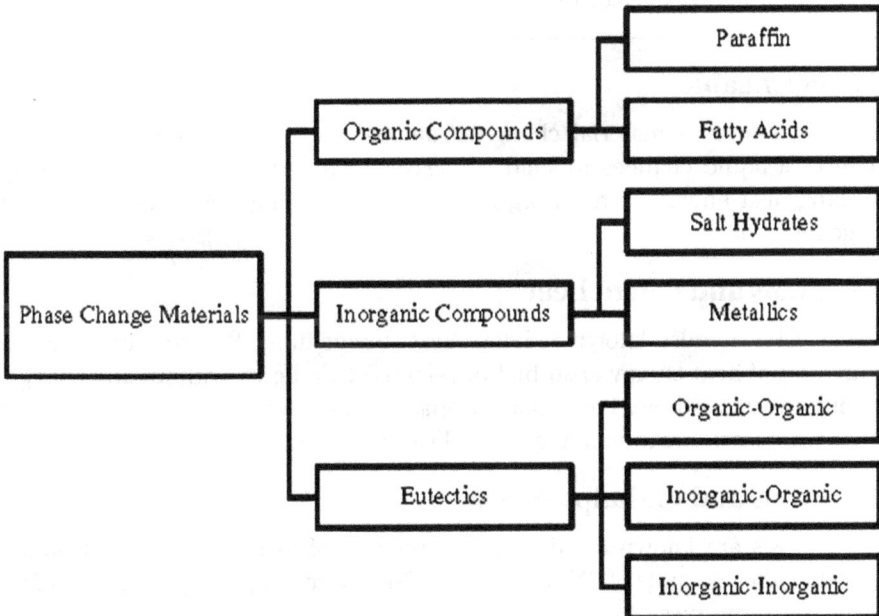

4.5.3. Applications of PCM

1. Cooling Packs
2. Thermasorb Capsules
3. Body Cooler
4. Bridge Warmer
5. NASA Dive Suit
6. Building Insulation

4.5.4. Comparison of different kinds of PCMs

Classification	Advantages	Disadvantages
Organic PCMs	1. Availability in a large temperature range 2. High heat of fusion 3. No supercooling 4. Chemically stable and recyclable 5. Good compatibility with other materials	1. Low thermal conductivity (around 0.2 W/m K) 2. Relative large volume change 3.Flammability
Inorganic PCMs	1.High heat of fusion 2. High thermal conductivity (around 0.5 W/m K) 3. Low volume change 4. Availability in low cost	1. Super cooling 2. Corrosion
Eutectics	1. Sharp melting Temperature 2. High volumetric thermal storage density	Lack of currently available test data of thermo-physical properties

4.5.5. Permeable

Whenever a material changes from solid to liquid it absorbs heat, and whenever a liquid changes to solid it releases heat. A material that is capable of absorbing heat energy or releasing heat energy, at a large-scale, is called phase-change material.

4.5.6. PCMs and Latent heat

PCMs are also known as latent heat storage units. By latent heat we mean the amount of heat energy absorbed or released by a body, without any change in temperature, as a whole. For instance, phase change from solid to liquid absorbs energy, whereas liquid to solid requires release of energy.

4.5.7. PCMs and Enthalpy of fusion

PCMs are known for their high enthalpy of fusion or heat of fusion. By segregating the two parts of ENTHALPY of FUSION, we can get a general idea of what is meant by this phrase,

1. ENTHALPY means the measure of the total energy of a thermodynamic system or body. It includes the internal energy, which is the energy

required to create a system, and the amount of energy required to make room for it by displacing its environment and establishing its volume and pressure.

2. FUSION which is also known as MELTING, is a physical process that results in the phase change of a substance from a solid to a liquid. The internal energy of a substance is increased, typically by the application of heat or pressure, resulting in a rise of its temperature to the melting point, at which the rigid ordering of molecular entities in the solid breaks down to a less-ordered state and the solid liquefies. An object that has melted completely is molten.

4.5.8. Classification

PCMs latent heat storage can be achieved through solid–solid, solid–liquid, solid–gas and liquid–gas phase change. However, the only phase change used for PCMs is the solid–liquid change.

4.5.9. Limitations

1. Liquid-gas phase changes are not practical for use as thermal storage due to the large volumes or high pressures required to store the materials when in their gas phase.

2. Liquid-gas transitions do have a higher heat of transformation than solid–liquid transitions.

3. Solid–solid phase changes are typically very slow and have a rather low heat of transformation.

4.5.10. Working of PCMs

1. Initially, the solid–liquid PCMs behave like sensible heat storage (SHS) materials; their temperature rises as they absorb heat.

4.5.11. Sensible heat storage material(SHS)

An SHS or Sensible Heat Storage material is a system that works on the principle of SENSIBLE HEAT, whereas sensible heat is a term that is used in contrast to the LATENT HEAT. Because in case of LATENT HEAT the system e. g, ice keeps on absorbing heat constantly and the temperature around it remains the same till it has changed its phase to liquid. However, in case of Sensible Heat the body with the absorption or release of heat also causes consistent change in temperature in the surrounding. Unlike conventional SHS, however, when PCMs reach the temperature at which they change phase (their melting temperature) they absorb large amounts of heat at an almost constant temperature. The PCM continues to absorb heat without a significant rise in temperature until all the material is transformed to the liquid phase. When the ambient temperature around a liquid material falls, the PCM solidifies, releasing its stored latent heat.

❖ Large number of PCMs are available in any required temperature range from –5 up to 190°C.

❖ Within the human comfort range of 20° to 30°C, some PCMs are very effective.

❖ They store 5 to 14 times more heat per unit volume than conventional storage materials such as water, masonry or rock.

4.5.12. Major types of PCMs

1. Organic PCMs

Paraffin (CnH_2n+2) and fatty acids ($CH_3(CH_2)2nCOOH$)

2. Inorganic PCMs

Salt hydrates (MnH_2O)

3. Eutectics

Organic-organic, organic-inorganic, inorganic-inorganic compounds

4. Hygroscopic materials

Many natural building materials are hygroscopic.

Selection criteria

While selecting a Phase Change Material, following characteristics should be kept in mind:

Thermodynamic properties

1. Melting temperature in the desired operating temperature range
2. High latent heat of fusion per unit volume
3. High specific heat, high density and high thermal conductivity
4. Small volume changes on phase transformation and small vapor pressure at operating temperatures to reduce the containment problem
5. Congruent melting

Kinetic properties

1. High nucleation rate to avoid super cooling of the liquid phase
2. High rate of crystal growth, so that the system can meet demands of heat recovery from the storage system
3. Chemical properties
4. Chemical stability
5. Complete reversible freeze/melt cycle
6. No degradation after a large number of freeze/melt cycle
7. Non-corrosiveness, non-toxic, non-flammable and non-explosive materials

Economic properties

1. Low cost
2. Availability

PCMs in textile clothing

These are smart fabrics. Put a warm hand on PCM fabric swatches and you can feel it for yourself, as the fabric actively draws the heat from your hand. Alternatively, put a cold hand on there and you'll feel it begin to get warmer. Phase change materials (PCM's) can keep you cool when it's hot and warm you up when you get too cold. Well, that's to say they can is you select the right. They can be used alone or in combination with other technologies to create passive cooling systems, PCM's have, unfortunately, previously been victims of their own hype: they promised a lot but early users were often disappointed with the performance level they actually delivered. Since then, hwever, new application methods mean that it's now possible to achieve significant and permanent heat regulation effects even under very demanding conditions.

Working in clothing

1. As we know PCMs are latent heat storage units, so the garments or apparel units made up of these are also HEAT STORAGE UNITS.
2. When a PCM garment is facing rise in temperature due to external or internal conditions, its solid phase encapsulations starts absorbing heat energy under a constant temperature and change to liquid phase, thus providing cooling effect to the user.
3. In case of freezing temperature or cold conditions, the liquid phase encapsulated apparel releases the stored energy under constant temperature, thus providing heat and soothing effect to the body.
4. American Society for Testing and Materials (ASTM), is an international standards organization that develops and publishes voluntary consensus technical standards for a wide range of materials, products, systems, and services. To measure the dynamic thermal performance of fabrics containing phase-change materials, a new standard is being developed by ASTM Committee D13 on Textiles.

Recent Developments in Textile Wet Processing

Wet processing of textiles uses large quantities of water, electrical and thermal energy. The present scenario calls for the conservation of energy or usage of low amount of energy. Water as solvent for chemicals is mostly used because of its abundant availability and low cost. Problems associated with usage of water are effluent generation and additional step is needed to dry the fabrics after each step. The amount of energy spent to remove the water is also huge adding to the woes of processors, making processing the weakest link among the entire textile chain. Various approaches on the several textile substrates have been experimented. None of these methods are commercially viable due to the inherent limitations. Solvent dyeing with different dyes, the use of ultrasonic waves and EM radiations are also one of the sources of getting energy which can be utilised in textile wet processing.

5.1. New technologies in textile wet processing

Conventional Textile Coloration and other wet processing with their inherent challenges are about to transform. As, after dyeing, the unspent dyestuffs remain in liquor, thus polluting the effluent. It leads to additional pollution of waste water. To eliminate the disadvantages, various new technologies have been recently developed and now ready to be implemented on a bulk scale. These are some of the revolutionary ways to advance the textile wet processing:

- ❖ Ultrasonic waves
- ❖ Microwaves
- ❖ Electrochemical dyeing
- ❖ Pre-treatments using plasma technology
- ❖ Waterless dyeing with Supercritical Carbon Dioxide (scCO2)
- ❖ Biotechnological catalytic bleaching
- ❖ Single stage preparatory process
- ❖ Foam finishing

5.1.1. Ultrasonic waves assisted textile processing

In recent decades, ultrasound has established an important place in different industrial processes and has started to revolutionise environmental protection. Ultrasonic represents a special branch of general acoustics, the science of mechanical oscillations of solids, liquids and gaseous media.

5.1.1.1 Ultrasonic

Sound waves have been classified into infra-sound (up to 16 Hz), audible sound (16 Hz - 16,000 Hz) and ultrasound, which include sound waves higher than audible sound with a frequency above approximately 16 kHz up to 106 kHz. With reference to the properties of human ear, high frequency inaudible oscillations are ultrasonic or supersonic. In other words, while the normal range of human hearing is in between 16 Hz and 16 kHz, ultrasonic frequencies lie between 20 kHz and 500 MHz.

5.1.1.2 Working of ultrasonic radiations

Unlike gases and liquid, in solids both longitudinal and transverse waves are transmitted. The effects of ultrasonics actually arise from the way in which sound is propagated through the medium. In liquids, longitudinal vibrations of molecules generate compressions and rare factions, i.e. areas of high and low local pressure. The latter results in the formation of cavities, i.e., very small vapor bubbles of 500 nm in size, which can collapse and cause shock waves through out the medium. The formation of cavitations depends on the frequency and intensity of waves, temperature and vapor pressure of the liquid. Cavitation is the principal physical phenomenon behind all the effects of ultrasound in most of the treatments. Cavitations refer to the formation, growth and collapse of vapour or gas bubbles under the influence of ultrasound.

If the bubbles collapse in the vicinity of a solid surface such as a textile material, it results in the formation of a high velocity micro jet with the velocities as high as 100 m/s - 150 m/s directed towards the solid surface. The two phenomena attributed to ultrasound are the rapid movement of liquids caused by variation of sonic pressure which subjects the solvent to compression and rarefaction and micro streaming. Simultaneous formation and collapsing of tiny air bubbles result in a large increase in pressure and temperature at microscopic level. Heat induced by the ultrasonic process is adequate for dyeing process and thus eliminates the need for external heating in many cases.

5.1.1.3 Use of ultrasonic radiation in textile processing

Ultrasonic method has been effectively utilised in various fabric preparation processes including desizing, scouring, bleaching, mercerisation and auxiliary processes like washing and laundering.

I. Desizing: Desizing of cotton and nylon fabrics under ultrasonic treatment results complete removal of oils used in the size recipe while the treatment without ultrasound shows residual oil stains. It was found that the use of degraded starch followed by ultrasonic desizing could lead to considerably energy saving as compared to conventional starch sizing and desizing. Fibre degradation is also reduced and final whiteness and wet ability of the fabric are same as those of without ultrasonic.

II. Scouring and bleaching: The scouring of wool in neutral and very light alkaline bath reduces the fibre damage and enhance rate of processing for peroxide bleaching of cotton fabric by using 20 KHz frequency and observed an increase in bleaching rate in required time. The degree of whiteness also increases as compared to that of conventionally bleached sample. Effect of ultrasonic in enzymatic scouring has been tested using both acidic pectinases and alkaline pectinases and found to have increased wettability of all treated samples both tests compared to the conventionally treated samples. Ultrasonic treatments help to reduce the processing and temperature required for a result comparable to the normal bleaching and subsequent dyeing processes in terms of absorbency and fastness properties.

III. Mercerisation: Ultrasound is used for mercerising 100 per cent cotton fabrics in the after treatment and speeds up the process up to 2-3 times. Ultrasonic also has been used for evaluating its impact on washing the fabrics and garments under the simulated stain conditions on 100 per cent PES and P/C (65/35) blends using the detergent of 1 g/L.

IV. Dyeing: The possibility of dyeing textile using ultrasound was started in 1941. The dyeing of cotton with direct dyes, wool with acid dyes, polyamide and acetate fibre with disperse dyes can be used. When ultrasound waves are absorbed in the liquid system the phenomenon of cavitation takes place. Cavitation can liberate entrapped gases from liquid or porous materials like textiles, dyebath, *etc.* The significant increases in rate of dyeing with disperse dyes on polyamide and acetate was obtained. Ultrasound is more beneficial to the application of water insoluble dyes to the hydrophobic fibres. Ultrasound irradiation also produces a greater evenness in color. The dyeing results are affected by frequency of ultrasound used. Frequency of 50 or 100 c/s produces no effect while frequency of 22 to175 Kc/s has been found to be most effective. Enzymatic treatments supplemented with ultrasonic energy resulted in shorter processing times, less consumption of expensive enzymes, less fibre damage, and better uniformity treatment to the fabric. The influence of ultrasound on dyeing is explained to have three-way effects:

❖ **Dispersion:** Breaking up of micelles and high molecular weight aggregates in to uniform dispersion in the dyebath.

❖ **Degassing:** Removal of dissolved or entrapped gases or air molecules from fibre capillaries and interstices at the cross over points of fibre in to liquid thereby facilitating a dye-fibre contact.

❖ **Diffusion:** Accelerating the rate of diffusion of dye inside the fibre by piercing the insulating layer covering the fibre and accelerating the interaction between dye and fibre. Effects 1 and II are promoted by the mechanical action of cavitation, while effect III is due to both the mechanical action and the heating of the fibre surface. In case of water soluble dyes, ultrasound constitutes mostly an effective means of mechanical agitation, whereas in case of pigments, which are not soluble in water, ultrasound provides means of pigment dispersion and penetration, which is not provided by the conventional method.

5.1.1.4 Effect of ultrasonic on fibres

Attempts have been made to analyse the effect of ultrasonic in dyeing processes on almost all types of fibres using direct, reactive, acid and disperse dyes. Ultrasonic waves accelerate the rate of diffusion of the dye inside the fibre with enhanced wetting of fibres. Acoustic irradiation of the liquor results in a higher and more uniform concentration of dyestuff on the fibre surface, making it available for ready diffusion into the fibre interior. The dyeing results are affected by the frequency of the ultrasound used. Irradiation at very low frequencies of the order of 50 or 100 cps produces no effects. Frequencies in the range between 22 and 175 KHz have been found to be most effective, the latter frequency being preferable for silk, wool and nylon.

5.1.1.5 Equipment for ultrasound

Generator and converter or cleaning bath are the two main components of ultrasound equipment. Generator converts 50 to 60 Hz alternate current to electrical energy of high frequency. This electrical energy is fed to the transducer where it is transformed to mechanical vibration. The transducer system vibrates longitudinally transmitting waves into liquid medium. As these waves propagate cavitation occurs. Prototype dyeing machine was designed for continuous dyeing of yam and fabric. The system mainly consists of the tank, transport system and microprocessor, which is used to monitor the process. Ultrasonic tank is of 92 x 60 cm dimensions and capacity up to 200 litres. Temperature can be varied up to 100°C by thermostatic control.

5.1.16 Potential advantages

The use of ultrasound in textile wet processing offers many potential advantages including energy saving by reduced processing temperature, reduced processing time, and lower consumptions of auxiliary chemicals and further processing enhancement by overall cost control. Other benefits include environmental improvements by reduced consumption of auxiliary chemicals, processing enhancement by allowing real-time control, slower overall processing costs, thereby increasing industry competitiveness.

5.1.2. Microwaves

Microwaves are electromagnetic waves whose frequency ranges from 1,000 MHz to 10,00,000 MHz. Microwaves are so called since they are defined in terms of their wavelength in the sense that micro refers to tiny. In other words the wavelengths of microwaves are short at the above range of frequency, typically from few centimeters to few millimeters. The higher frequency edge of microwave borders on the infrared and visible light region of the spectrum.

5.1.2.1 Microwave dyeing

Microwave dyeing takes into account only the dielectric and the thermal properties. The dielectric property refers to the intrinsic electrical properties that affect the dyeing by dipolar rotation of the dye and influences the microwave field upon the dipoles. The aqueous solution of dye has two components which are polar, in the high frequency microwave field oscillating at 2,450 MHz. It influences the vibrational energy in the water molecules and the dye molecules.

The heating mechanism is through ionic conduction, which is a type of resistance heating. Depending on the acceleration of the ions through the dye solution, it results in collision of dye molecules with the molecules of the fibre. The mordant helps and affects the penetration of the dye and also the depth to which the penetration takes place in the fabric. This makes microwave superior to conventional dyeing techniques.

5.1.3. Electrochemical dyeing

The vat and sulphur dyes are insoluble in water, therefore for their application, it is necessary to convert them into water-soluble form using suitable reducing agent and alkali. The conventional reducing agents, which reduce the dyestuff, result in non-regenerable oxidised byproducts that remain in the bath. The used dye bath cannot be recycled because the reducing power of these chemicals cannot be regained. The disposal of the dye bath and the washing water cause various problems due to the non ecofriendly nature of the decomposed products. Maximum attention must therefore be paid from the ecological standpoint to the necessary reducing agent for these dyes. Electrochemical dyeing is still in the laboratory stage but could become the dyeing process of the future of the vat, indigo and sulphur according to BASF, a leading dyestuff manufacturing company. Electrons from the electric current replace Electrochemical dyeing in which chemical reducing agents, and effluent contaminating substances can be dispensed with altogether.

Different reducing agents used for vat and shulphur dyes are:

5.1.3.1 Reducing agent for the vat dyes

Sodium dye thionite is the universal and mainly used reducing agent for the vat dyes. It is also known as sodium hydrosulphite. It reduces the entire vat dye at the temp range 300-600 degree Celsius and above. Sodium dithionite dissociates properly and liberates nascent hydrogen. Sodium dithionite is very unstable and get decomposed (oxidative) and thermally to several byproducts. Some are acidic in nature. The stability of the alkaline solution of sodium dithionite decreased with increased with temperature; increased surface exposed to the air and decreased agitation bath.

5.1.3.2 Vat dyeing by electrochemical method

Dyestar has patented an electrochemical dyeing process that it developed jointly with the textile machinery manufacturer Thies GmbH & Co and the Institute of Textile Chemistry and Textile Physics at University of Innsbruck in Dornbirn, Austria. According to the company, the process uses an electric current instead of chemical reducing agents, giving it a number of technical, economic and ecological benefits. Dyestar has developed a vat dye, Indanthrane blue E-BC, specifically for this electrochemical dyeing process. The dye liquor used in electrochemical dyeing with Indanthrane blue E-BC can be reused in an unlimited number of times and contamination of dye house effluent is close to zero.

There are two methods by means of which electrochemical dyeing can be carried out:

a. Direct electrochemical dyeing

In case of direct electrochemical dyeing technique, organic dyestuff has been directly reduced by contact between dye and electrode. However in practice, the dyestuff is partially reduced by using conventional reducing agent and then complete dye reduction is achieved by electrochemical process for complete reduction which facilitates the improved stability of the reduced dye. In order to start the process, an initial amount of the leuco dye has to be generated by a conventional reaction, i.e. by adding a small amount of a soluble reducing agent. Once the reaction has set in, it is not needed anymore and further process is self sustaining. The system is found successful in case of sulphur dyes. However, concentration of the dye required to get a specific shade is higher than the conventional reducing process. In such a system, a dyestuff particle must come into contact with the electrode surface in order to get reduced. However, the atmosphere oxygen, present in the dye solution, immediately reoxidises the dyestuff has no protective capacity. Also, since the dye itself must be reduced at the surface of the cathode, cathode area should be large which itself is a constraint.

b. Indirect electrochemical dyeing

Thomas Bechtold patented indirect electrochemical dye reduction method in 1993. Here, the dye is not directly reduced at the electrode. Rather, a reducing agent is added that reduces the dye in the conventional manner which in turn gets oxidised after dye reduction. The oxidised reducing agent is subsequently reduced at the cathode surface, which is then further available for dye reduction. This cycle is continuously repeated during the dyeing operation. In electrochemistry, the agent, which under goes reduction and oxidation cycles, is known as reversible redox system and is called a mediator. Thus, in the system, the dye reduction does not take place due to direct contact of dyestuff with the cathode, like in direct electrochemical reduction, but it takes place through the mediator which gets repeatedly reduced due to the contact with the cathode. Therefore this system is known as indirect electrochemical dyeing. The object of the reversible redox system primarily in the first place is to generate a continuous regenerable reduction potential in the dye liquor. Therefore addition of conventional reducing agent is not essential and therefore there is no accumulation of decomposition products of the reducing agents takes place in the indirect electrochemical dyeing.

The electrochemical dyeing appears simple because after dyeing cycle, the unexhausted dye gets precipitated by air oxidation and can be removed by filtration. After the dye removal, the color containing the mediator, ligand and alkali can be recycled for subsequent dyeing operation. This appears to be most important feature in the terms of the cost and the environment friendliness of the process.

Points to be considered in indirect electro chemical dyeing process:

❖ The actual reduction of the dye should be carried separately into electrochemical cell and the reduced dye is then circulated separately into a conventional dyeing unit.

❖ To keep the dye in reduced form it is necessary to reduce the oxidised mediator at the cathode.

❖ The design of the cell should be such that the cathode should have the maximum surface area available for the reduction of mediator.

❖ A three dimensional electrode with large surface area occupying small place in electrochemical cell should be designed.

5.1.4. Plasma technology in textile processing

Plasma has been known from the dawn of mankind from its natural appearance in lightning displays, the solar corona and the northern lights.

5.1.4.1 Plasma

Plasma is the fourth state of matter, after solids, liquids and gases, and this fourth state was first proposed by Sir William Crooke in 1879 as a result of his experiments in the passage of electricity through gases. The word plasma comes originally from a Greek term meaning something formed, fabricated and molded and was first used by Irving Langmuir in 1929.

The physical definition of 'plasma' is an ionised gas with an essentially equal density of positive and negative charges. And today the term is recognised as being generated by electrical discharges through a gas and it consists of a mixture of positive and negative ions, electrons, free radicals, ultraviolet radiation and many different electronically excited molecules.

5.1.4.2 Principle of plasma application

The plasma atmosphere consists of free electrons, radicals, ions, UV-radiations and lot of different excited particles in dependence of the used gas. Thus, gas plasma treatment differs in nature according to the specific gas or gases, e.g. air, ammonia, argon, *etc.* Any gas plasma contains a complex mixture of species that can interact with textile fibres placed in the vicinity of the plasma, and this can lead to a variety of fibre-surface treatments. The nature of the gas composition, the type of textile fibre, and machine parameters such as the pressure within the plasma chamber, the treatment temperature and time, and the frequency and power of the electrical supply, can be used to vary the type and degree of fibre modification. Different reactive species in plasma chamber interact with the substrate surface cleaning, modification or coating occur dependent of the used parameter. Furthermore the plasma process can be carried out in different manners. The substrate can be treated directly in the plasma zone. The substrate can be positioned outside the plasma; this process is called remote process. The substrate can be achieved in the plasma followed by a subsequent grafting. The substrate can be treated with a polymer solution or gas which will be fixed or polymerised by a subsequent plasma treatment.

5.1.4.3 Plasma equipment

Plasma may be generated in the laboratory using non-electrical discharges, e.g. Thermal methods, shock waves, chemical reactions of high specific energy, nuclear radiation or irradiation by high-energy photons, gamma rays or alpha particles. However, for plasma treatment of textiles only electrical-discharge techniques are used. Plasma is a partially ionised gas containing ions, electrons, atoms and neutral species. To enable the gas to be ionised in a controlled and qualitative manner, the process is carried in vacuum conditions. A vacuum vessel is first pumped down via rotary and roots blowers, sometimes in conjunction with high-vacuum pumps, to a low to medium vacuum pressure in the range of 10-2 to 10-3 mbar. The gas is then introduced into the vessel by means of mass flow controllers and valves. Although many gases can be used, commonly selected gases or mixture of gases for plasma treatment of polymers include oxygen, argon, nitrous oxide, tetrafluoromethane and air.

5.1.4.4 Plasma application on textile substrate

For the pretreatment of textile substrate

The application of sizing agent to warp yarns prior to weaving is essential for high weaving efficiency in the production of most fabrics. Starch-based products carboxymethyl cellulose (CMC) and polyvinyl alcohol (PVA) are most frequently used sizes for cotton yarns. It is very important that these sizes should be removed by wet processing prior to the dyeing and finishing of the woven fabrics. Because of the resulting desizing waste there has recently been great interest in physico-chemicals methods. The weight loss for plasma-treated fabric increased dramatically with the exposure time of less than 5 minutes in the plasma chamber, however, it increased slowly after the plasma treatment time exceeded 5 minutes. The effect of plasma treatment on the removal of PVA was studied. The effect of varying plasma treatment time on the PVA removal was apparent. Even treatment duration of 0.5 minute removed 3.48 per cent PVA on cotton.

Plasma application for dyeing of textile substrate

Dyeability of Cotton Substrate: It has been reported that plasma treatment on cotton in presence of air or argon gas increases its water absorbency. This report was concerned with the effect of air and oxygen plasma on the rate and extent of dye uptake of Chloramine Fast Red K on cotton print cloth. The effect of plasma treatment in two different gas atmospheres (air and oxygen) for different treatment times was studied by applying 2 per cent of Chloramine Fast Red K. The effect of plasma treatment in air and oxygen appears to increase both the rate of dyeing and the direct dye uptake in the absence of electrolyte in the dye bath. Oxygen treatment is more effective than air plasma treatment. This shows that the increase in the rate and extent of dye uptake for the direct dye studied depends more on the oxygen component of the air than on the nitrogen component, which supports an oxidative mechanism of attack on the cotton.

5.1.5. Supercritical carbon dioxide

Water is a valuable raw material which is not unlimitedly available. It must be protected by appropriate legal measures. Usage of water as solvent for chemicals is mostly because of its abundant availability and low cost. Problems associated with usage of water are effluent generation and additional step is needed to dry the fabrics after each step. The amount of energy spent to remove the water is also huge. The unspent dyestuffs remain in liquor, thus polluting the effluent. It leads to additional pollution of waste water. To eliminate the disadvantages it is proposed that certain gases can replace water as solvating medium. High pressure and temperature are needed to dissolve the dyes. Of all the gases being possible of converted into super critical fluids, CO_2 is the most versatile and prominently used. Because of their high diffusion rates and low viscosities that allow the dye to penetrate into the fibre. Moreover, by reducing the pressure at the end of the process, dye and CO_2 can be recycled.

5.1.5.1 Carbion dioxide CO_2

Prominent substances exhibiting super critical phases are CO_2, H_2O and Propane, of which CO2 is the second most abundant and second least costly solvent. Low temperature and pressure are needed to convert carbon dioxide gas into super critical fluid. In the supercritical state CO_2 exhibits very low viscosity and surface tension properties. Supercritical CO_2 is one of the most popular fluids currently used in manufacturing processes.

Following are the benefits which make CO_2 most suitable for this purpose.

- ❖ Abundantly available
- ❖ Recovery and reuse is easier
- ❖ Easily Handelable and environment friendly
- ❖ Non toxic, non hazardous and low cost
- ❖ No waste generation
- ❖ Chemically inert

5.1.5.2 Supercritical dye system

It represents the presence of three components: the textile substrate, dye stuff and the super critical fluid. The dyestuff is dissolved in the supercritical fluid, transferred to, absorbed by and diffused into the fibre.

5.1.5.3 Dyeing process

Any gas above its critical temperature retains the free mobility of the gaseous state but with increasing pressure its density will increase towards that of a liquid. Supercritical fluids are highly compressed gases and combine valuable properties of both liquid and gas. Supercritical fluids have solvent power similar to a light hydrocarbon for most solutes. Solubility increases with increasing density (i.e., with increasing pressure). However, fluorinated compounds are often more soluble in CO_2 than in hydrocarbons, which increased solubility, is important for polymerisation. A liquid can be converted to a supercritical fluid by increasing the temperature and consequently its vapor pressure and simultaneously with increasing pressure. A closed system thus reaches the supercritical state, where no boundary between the liquid and gaseous state can be distinguished. The dyeing takes place in following steps

❖ Dissolution of dye in CO_2
❖ Transport to the fibres
❖ Adsorption of dye on fibre surface and finally
❖ Diffusion of dye into the fibre takes place

The sample to be dyed is wrapped around a perforated stainless steel tube and mounted inside the autoclave around the stirrer. Dyestuff powder is placed at the bottom of the vessel and the apparatus is sealed, purged with gaseous CO_2 and preheated. When it reaches the working temperature, CO_2 is isothermally compressed to the chosen working pressure under constant stirring. Pressure is maintained for a dyeing period of 60 minutes and afterwards released. The CO_2 and excess dyes are separated and recycled. After this dyeing procedure, the dry sample is removed and rinsed with acetone if necessary to remove the adhering residual dye.

5.1.5.4 Effect of temperature and pressure on supercritical dyeing

The influence of temperature on the dyeing is mainly due to the increase in the diffusion rate of dyes in the polymer and thus affects the dyeing time. Pressure regulates the solubility of the dye stuff. The diffusion coefficients of the dye dissolved in the supercritical medium are higher than in water, leading to generally very short dyeing time. At low temperature, the solubility of the dye stuff in CO_2 is high and with low pressure and high temperature the dye content is small but its penetration into the fibre is facilitated. Since dyeing virtually takes place from gaseous phase, whereby the dyestuff is homogenously distributed, a high degree of levelness is achieved. For some fabrics extensive extraction of spinning oils should be avoided due to undesirable hardening of the handle of the fabric. The aim of extraction II with cold CO_2 at the end of dyeing process is to remove the unfixed dye and simultaneously decrease the temperature as fast as possible below the glass transition temperature to avoid the extraction of fixed dye from the fibre.

Any increase in pressure subsequently results, increase in dielectric constant and the dissolving power to a greater extent. Carbon dioxide is frequently used as a solvent because of some inherent advantages associated with the system like, non-toxic, non-corrosive and non-hazardous nature; CO_2 is produced commercially and can be transported easily. The critical points of the CO_2 can be achieved easily compared to other gases. The dissolved dyestuff available for diffusion into the boundary layers in the supercritical fluid is absorbed and diffuses into the fibres. The state of the dyestuff in a super critical solution can virtually be described as gaseous. Supercritical CO_2 has almost a plasticising effect which accelerates the diffusion processes by increasing the chain mobility of the polymeric molecules. This means that it will be absorbed by the fibre at a rate comparable to the high diffusion rates corresponding to that of a gas. The distribution dyestuff-fluid can be continuously shifted in favor of the polymer until after expansion of the gas to standard pressure the solubility in the fluid will be equal to zero, where a theoretical exhaustion level of 100 per cent is achieved.

5.1.5.5 Uses of Supercritical CO_2

Earlier supercritical CO_2 was tried for dry cleaning process but due to the damage to the buttons liquid CO_2 was preferred.It is used as a medium for extracting materials like natural wax, paraffin wax, knitting oil from fibres, yarns and fabrics. Another application is the sterilisation and disinfection of textiles and related material in the medical field.

5.1.5.6 Comparison with conventional dyeing process

In conventional method of dyeing, water, dyes, and other auxiliaries are used to enhance the efficiency of dyeing process. The cost of waste water treatment and of arranging water of acceptable quality is becoming serious concerns. Either the water available is too hard or not available in sufficient amount or therefore dyeing plants cannot be set up at some places. Compared to this, use of supercritical CO_2 completely avoids the use of water and other auxiliaries, thus creating no effluent. Drying is also not required as CO_2 is released in gaseous state. CO_2 can also be recycled up to 90 per cent and energy required is about 80 per cent less compared to conventional dyeing. Dyeing is only carried on for 2 hours compared to 3-4 hrs of conventional dyeing.

Advantages

- ❖ Elimination of water treatment and water pollution
- ❖ No need of drying textiles
- ❖ Gives good rubbing fastness
- ❖ Dyeing occurs with high degree of levelness
- ❖ CO_2 is non toxic obtained from natural resources and can be easily recycled in dyeing process
- ❖ Dyeing houses may be started on sites where there is water scarcity

Disadvantages

a. High pressure and high temperature are observed during the process
b. The system requires a lot of money

5.1.6. Peracetic acid (PAA) bleaching an eco-friendly alternative

Any substitute to the traditional bleaching agent NaOCl, should be a product with comparable redox potential. In case of low temperature bleaching it has been introduced peracids as stronger oxidising agents than hydrogen peroxide. PAA as a bleaching agent has been used for different fibres like cotton, flax, nylon 4 –9. The rate of decomposition and consumption of PAA vary over a range of bleaching temperature at different pH with varieties of alkalis. PAA consumption is slow when sodium hydroxide (NaOH) is used as an activator, at different values of pH and temperature, whereas consumption is quicker and rapid with inclusion of magnesium carbonate. At higher pH and temperature, PAA decomposes spontaneously to produce acetic acid and oxygen.

Fabrics treated with PAA at neutral pH at room temperature for about an hour followed by alkaline peroxide bleaching at 90°C have shown a brightness of greater than 90 Berger units, significantly with less fibre damage and crease marks. PAA is used for the removal of heat setting discoloration from nylon, carried out at pH 6.0 - 7.5 for about an hour at 80°C using 0.3 per cent solution. The similar process also could be used for viscose rayon, secondary acetate and triacetate materials.

5.1.6.1 Implementation of single stage preparatory process

Single stage preparatory process using hydrogen peroxide has been developed successfully for starch and acrylic-base sized textile materials previously. In such processes, caustic soda provides required alkalinity for scouring and activation of hydrogen peroxide and when activated, hydrogen peroxide degrades the sizing materials at lower temperature and at higher temperature, bleaching occur along with completion of desizing. Higher alkalinity at elevated temperature produces efficient scouring action. A self-emulsifiable solvent system of bleaching has been developed to combine the three different processes involved in the preparatory process. The system uses a high proportion of water, very low levels of solvents and hydrogen peroxide. The presence of hydrogen peroxide helps both desizing and bleaching and the emulsified solvent results in the scouring of cotton fabric. Since the system involves very low quantity of solvent content, need for a solvent recovery plant is obviated. In the case of sodium chloride (NaCl)- hydrogen peroxide (H2O2) system, free radical mechanism (Mechanism-2) is responsible for the bleaching action. Various free radicals created during the treatment resulted in disintegration and destruction of foreign matters present in the cotton. The bleaching effect is more distinct with peroxide than sodium chlorite, even at the higher concentrations. Presence of co-oxidants impedes the decomposition of each other, especially at their lower concentrations. The reactions under alkaline medium are initiated as chain reaction by the production of different free radical in different steps.

The HO• and HOO• radicals react with the chlorite ions and, as the result, a reaction chain is perpetuated as suggested as:

$$ClO_2 + HO• ------> ClO- + H_2O$$
$$ClO_2 + HO• ------> ClO_2 + HO_2-$$

$$2CiO_2 \longrightarrow C1O\text{-} + C1O_3\text{-}$$
$$C1O_2 + C1O \longrightarrow C1O\bullet - C1O_2\text{-}$$
$$C1O\bullet + C1O\text{-} + HO_2 \longrightarrow C1_2 + O_2 + HO\bullet$$

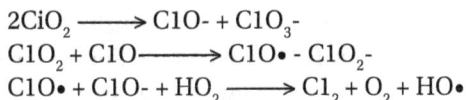

These free radicals enhance the bleaching effect of NaCl by H_2O_2 when used at their higher concentration. Thus created free radicals seem to disintegrate the impurities and destroy the coloring matters of the cotton. In case of the hypochlorite-solvent assisted single stage preparatory process, the whiteness index and tensile strength exhibit approximately a linear relationship with available chlorine in sodium hypochlorite solution at various treatment at a time range from 45 to 225 min. Better wetting time is obtained at the scouring agent concentration of 8 per cent at a temperature of 50°C – 55°C, which is closer to the cloud point of the non-ionic emulsifier used in the recipe. In the peroxide-alkali process, absence of either sodium hydroxide or hydrogen peroxide in the peroxide based process results very low weight loss, indicating very low efficiency.

5.1.7. Foam finishing

Conservation of water and energy has been the centre of research during the past and today also and foam finishing process can be used to achieve 80 per cent of water consumption, the energy consumption by 60-65 per cent in the form of gas, electricity depending upon the type of finishing treatment used, obnoxious gases and their related pollution can be minimised. The wet processing of textile materials includes highly energy consuming operations, approximately to 80 per cent of total energy requirement of all the operations. Out of this, about 66 per cent of the energy is consumed in heating and evaporation of water from the fibres. Invariably, the liquor retained in the fabric is distributed within and between the fibres in the form of capillary liquid in the available spaces between the yarns and also on the surface of the textile material, i.e., surface bound water. Squeezing the fabric between the nips eliminate the excess liquor available on the surface of the fabric and the interstices of the yarns, which depends on the nip pressure, hardness of rubber, roller diameter and machine speed or fabric speed. The concept of low add-on is based on the controlled transfer of a reduced quantity of liquor from a dipping roller to the fabrics. Moreover foam application is different from the low add-on technique since air is used to dilute the liquor, which is not the case in the earlier ones. In the foam process the liquor is diluted using the air instead of water that is normally used to apply the chemicals over the textile materials.

In foam finishing, most of the water is replaced by air, which leads to a reduction of energy requirements in the drying processes resulting in substantial savings in energy cost. Foam is a colloidal system comprising of mass of gas bubbles dispersed in the liquid continuum. Foam can be generated by mechanical air blowing, through excess agitation or chemically by introduction of foaming agents or combination of these methods. The relative proportions of air and liquid phases in the foam are designated by blow ratio. Foam stability, density and diameters are the important parameters that need constant attention.

A varying bubble size represents an unbalanced bath density. Foam density in general, varies between 0.14 g/cc – 0.07 g/cc for the foam finishing and 0.33 g/cc – 0.20 g/cc in the foam printing. The selection of the density of the foam depends on the fabric weight and needs to be increased with increasing fabric weight. Foam viscosity depends on the foam density and viscosity of the un-foamed liquor. Increase in foam viscosity results increased foam stability. Bubbles with smaller size are more stable than bigger bubble size and the bubble diameter ranges, generally, from 0.001 mm – 2.0 mm depending on the generation systems. Bubbles or foams, inherently, do not thrive in higher energy environment since higher energy levels results in the destability of the foam. Destabilisation of the foam is also caused by creation of the faults in the foam structure at the air/liquid/air interface. The destruction of foam after application on to the fabrics can be achieved by conventional padding or vacuum application or combination of both.

Usage: Foam application technique can be used in the fabric preparation, dyeing and printing, DP finish, softening, soil-release finish, water, oil repellent finish, FR finish, anti-static finish, mercerisation, *etc.* The foam can be applied either on one or both sides of the fabrics. Horizontal padder, kiss roller coating, knife over the roller coating, knife on air system and slot applicator system are commonly employed in foam applications. The chief advantages of foam application techniques with foam finishing treatment reduce the payback period to as low as six months to two years.

5.1.8. Use of enzymes

Textile processing has benefited greatly in both environmental impact and product quality through the use of enzymes. As using of enzymes in textile processing and after-care is already the best established example of the application of biotechnology too. The principal enzymes applied in textile industry are hydrolases and oxidoreductases. The group of hydrolases includes amylases, cellulases, proteases, pectinases and lipases/esterases. Amylases were the only enzymes applied in textile processing until the 1980s. These enzymes are still used to remove starch-based sizes from fabrics after weaving. Cellulases have been employed to enzymatically remove fibrils and fuzz fibres, and have also successfully been introduced to the cotton textile industry.

Further applications have been found for these enzymes to produce the aged look of denim and other garments. The potential of proteolytic enzymes was assessed for the removal of wool fibre scales, resulting in improved anti-felting behavior. However, an industrial process has yet to be realised. Esterases have been successfully studied for the partial hydrolysis of synthetic fibre surfaces, improving their hydrophobicity and aiding further finishing steps. Besides hydrolytic enzymes, oxido reductases have also been used as powerful tools in various textile-processing steps. Catalases have been used to remove H_2O_2 after bleaching, reducing water consumption. Enzymes have also been widely used in domestic laundering detergents since the 1960s such as proteases which used for removing grass, blood, egg, sweat stains and Lipases used for Lipstick, butter, salad oil, sauces *etc.* Future developments in the field of textile after-care also include treatments to reverse wool shrinkage as well as alternatives to dry cleaning. On the other hand, Natural and enhanced microbial processes have been used for many years to treat waste materials and effluent streams from the textile industry. They include color removal from dyestuff effluent and the handling of toxic wastes including PCPs, insecticides and heavy metals. These are not only difficult to remove by conventional biological or chemical treatment but they are also prone to 'poison' the very systems used to treat them.

5.1.8.1 Cellulase for look, surface and hand modification

Cellulase enzymes were first introduced after decades of amylase usage as an industry standard for desizing processes. During the 1970s, the popularity of denim garments increased as new garment wet processes changed denim's look and feel from the hard, dark blue garments used as workwear into soft and smooth fashion items with an abraded look. Surprisingly, this look, first achieved by using pumice stones, also can be attained using cellulase enzymes. Cellulases loosen the surface fibres of the denim garment so that mechanical action in a washing machine breaks the surface to remove the indigo dye, revealing the white core of the ring-dyed yarns. The first cellulase products for this application were introduced in the 1980s, and today, most denim garments are 'stonewashed' using cellulases, either alone or in combination with a reduced amount of stones. The introduction of cellulases resulted in increased washing capacity for the laundries, and reduced damage to garments as well as to washing machines, in addition to diminishing environmental effects from pumice stone mining and disposal of used pumice.

5.1.8.2 Catalse for hydrogen peroxide removal

Today's textile processing industry uses a lot of hydrogen peroxide for bleaching of greige goods before dyeing or printing. After the bleaching process, the residual peroxide in the bath needs to be removed before the fabric enters the dyeing process, as the presence of peroxide changes the dye shade and causes an uneven dyeing result. Traditionally, peroxide removal has been done using several consecutive rinses with plentiful water, or using reducing chemicals such as bisulphite to break down the peroxide. Both methods are unreliable and call for high water consumption. A more modern way to remove peroxide involves the use of a catalase enzyme, which breaks down hydrogen peroxide into water and molecular oxygen. The advantage of this process is theend products are natural to the environment and do not disturb the dyeing process. Also, the catalase enzyme itself is very specific: When the peroxide is gone, the enzyme does not react with anything else, and thus there is no need to remove or inactivate it. The use of catalases has been the fastest-growing enzyme application in textiles in recent years.

5.1.8.3 Pectinases for cotton pretreatment

Today, efforts within the textile industry seem to focus on replacing traditional natural-fibre scouring processes with enzyme-based solutions. As the purpose of scouring is to remove natural impurities — such as polymeric substances like pectins, waxes and xylomannans, among others — from cotton or other natural fibres, there are plenty of enzymes that can act on such impurities. Alkaline pectinase, which loosens fibre structure by removing pectins between cellulose fibrils and eases the wash-off of waxy impurities, is the key enzyme for a bioscouring process. Other enzymes including cellulases, hemicellulases, proteases and lipases have been tested; but at present, the only commercial bioscouring enzyme products are based on pectinases.

Compared to the conventional alkaline boil-off, an efficient bioscouring process provides many advantages, such as reduced water and wastewater costs, reduced treatment time and lower energy consumption because of lower treatment temperature. Moreover, the weight loss in fabric is reduced, and fabric quality is improved with a superior hand and reduced strength loss.

However, there are several obstacles in the way of successfully commercialising the bioscouring process, primarily its inability to remove motes – the remainders of cottonseed fragments. Thus, a separate bleaching step would be needed after the bioscouring process. On the other hand, the alkaline boil-off can be combined with simultaneous peroxide bleaching to efficiently remove the motes. As motes are not acceptable on fabrics other than those that will be dyed to dark shades, bioscouring will have limited usage unless a simultaneous mote-removal process is developed.

5.1.8.4 Fluorocarbons

Fluorocarbon-based chemical products are in a continuous review due to the halogen content. Some years ago PFOA-based products were common in some industries (included plastic, toys and also textile resins and finishing products). Currently, PFOA resins are being rejected in the textile industry and C6-based (even C4) fluorocarbons are growing as the most common chemical products for liquid repellency finishing.

Other important trend in this field is the synthesis of finishing products with a drying/curing low temperature (120-130ºC instead of 150-160ºC) in order to be capable to process thermo-sensitive textile materials like PP or Elasthane, and also trying to reduce energy consumption of the oven.

5.1.8.5 Flame retardants (FR)

Main current trends of FRs finishes are focused in the use of halogen-free flame retardants (HFFRs) like nitrogen- and phosphorus-based compounds including organophosphored chemicals. Use of chemical products based on aluminium trihydroxide is growing, too. Chlorinated short chain FR compounds are PBTs (persistent, bioaccumulative and toxic) and endocrine disruptors (cause sex changes in aquatic animals) and are already restricted in the EU. Antimony oxide, like the halogen FRs, it is being restricted in the EU.

Phosphorus (P) and/or nitrogen (N)-based flame retardants: N-P's are increasingly used as replacements for halogen flame retardants and can be equally effective in some types of end applications when a high class of flame resistance is required. In general they are less persistent in the environment than brominated flame retardants but more testing is required to determine whether they pose a risk to health or the environment. They are the main compounds currently used in the textile finishing industry.

Other types of FRs. There are several other types of flame retardant used as solid powders and additives in smaller quantities, which are suitable to obtain good FR properties on textiles (mainly for fiber extrusion purposes; less options due to processing problems in the field of textile finishing). These could include melamine based compounds, borates and special nano-additives like carbon nano-tubes (CNTs) or nano-clays which FR properties and toxicity must be carefully tested.

Safety and health issues are also important in current trends for using FRs. Development and application of FRs with a very low content of formaldehyde is being reported in the textile industry to avoid skin injuries (e.g. allergies) caused by finished textiles; formaldehyde content must be taken into account as it is a compound considered as pre-carcinogen. Presence of free formaldehyde is common on finished textiles when the curing/polymerizing step is shorter than optimal conditions (less curing time or less temperature than recommended). Its content on textiles is assessed by Oekotex Standard-100 with some classes depending the end-use of the fabric (in general terms, formaldehyde content must be less than 20 ppm).

5.1.8.6 Antimicrobials

Current trends for using antimicrobial chemicals on textile finishing are still mainly silver-based compounds (they are specially recommended for treating textiles against bacteria). Other compounds like quaternary ammonium with modified organo-silane groups are also largely employed. An alternative to Triclosan could be chitosan-based compounds; on the other hand, an alternative to silver-based compounds could be chemicals with zinc (Zn) or copper (Cu). In any case, antimicrobial textile finishing should reach specific requirements due to their contact with living cells/organisms:

- Wide range of action.

- Easy application.

- Durability.

- Excellent skin compatibility.

5.1.8.7 UV protection

Products being used as UV-barriers are chemicals containing chromophores absorbing radiation or are particles with capabilities to disperse the electromagnetic radiation. Compounds like benzotriazoles, feniltrazines, benzophenones... are very effective for this purpose (even for other industrial end-applications like protection for plastics, cosmetics or sun-protectors for the skin). Current trends in this field are referred to use micro/nano-compounds based on TiO_2 and/or ZnO as UV-protectors; however, chemicals named above are mainly used in this moment.

5.1.8.8 Better touch/handle and softeners

Current trends on textile finishing to modify and to improve touch/handle are focused on nano-silicones, development and application of polyurethanes (PU) with a wide range of hardness and self-cross-linking behaviour, resins with lower drying/curing temperature than usual and resins with a very low emission level of free formaldehyde.

5.1.8.9 Wrinkle-free and easy care

A cross-linker which has been most frequently used until now in the industrial durable press finishing of cotton fabrics is dimethyloldihydroxyethyl urea (DMDHDU) which forms ether-type cross-linkages with the hydroxyl group of the cellulose. However, this cross-linker generates high levels of formaldehyde harmful to the human body, and thus, is currently used in a limited manner. Currently, there are actively progressed studies on polycarboxylic acids, which form ester-type cross-linkages with the hydroxyl group of the cellulose and do not generate formaldehyde. Meanwhile, although glyoxal is used in the synthesis of DMDHEU, it may also give excellent wrinkle-free performance by itself. Moreover, glyoxal has various advantages as compared to other cross-linkers. First, it has low costs and thus allows the finishing costs of fabrics to be reduced. Also, it is supplied in a highly stable aqueous solution, and thus, considerably easily handled. In addition, it has little or no poisonous character, and thus, can be used as a cross-linker having no harmful effect on the human body. However, when aluminium salt is used as a catalyst in durable press finishing using glyoxal as a cross-linker, fabrics can give excellent wrinkle-free performance but could be disadvantageous as serious reductions in the strength and whiteness of fabrics can be caused. Safety and health issues on wrinkle-free finishing compounds are mainly referred to the formaldehyde content on textiles finished with these compounds. Presence of free formaldehyde is common on finished textiles when the curing/polymerizing step is shorter than optimal conditions (less curing time or less temperature than recommended). Formaldehyde causes skin injuries (e.g. allergies) and is also considered as pre-carcinogen. Its content is assessed on textiles by Oekotex Standard-100 with some classes depending the end-use of the fabric (in general terms, formaldehyde content must be less than 20 ppm).

5.1.8.10 Electrical conductivity on textiles

Electrical conductivity on fabrics through finishing processes could be obtained by coating processes being the basis for the development of new and technical applications for textiles. To achieve this special functionality, 3 main pathways can be followed:

> ❖ Inclusion of micro/nanoadditives intrinsically electroconductive on a water-based polymeric resin. A current trend is the research and use of particles like carbon nanotubes (CNTs) for several textiles applications including finishing processes. CNTs coatings can be

developed if nanoparticles are properly dispersed in order to avoid aggregates through knife coating and transfer processes. Metallic micro/nanoparticles like copper could be also used for this purpose.

❖ Use of conductive polymers. Formulation and application of special polymers with conductive properties like polypyrrole (PPy), polyaniline (PANI) or polythiophene (PEDOT or poly-3,4-ethylenedioxythiophene) using finishing techniques like knife coating, printing o padding is also a current trend in the textile industry.

❖ Use of electro-conductive inks. The field of the "printed electronics" on flexible substrates is one of the most innovative markets for technological developments where the textile industry is currently involved. Through the application and use of electro-conductive inks (silver-based but also conductive polymer-based) with special composition that are also applied under special processing conditions for drying/curing, some electro-conductive textiles could be developed (e.g. from heatable elements to electroluminescent textiles). These inks can be applied with conventional printing techniques like screen printing but advanced technologies like inkjet printing are starting to be used with specially formulated inks.